Investigating Science with Young Children

Rosemary Althouse

**TEACHERS
COLLEGE
PRESS**

Teachers College, Columbia University
New York and London

Published by Teachers College Press, 1234 Amsterdam Avenue, New York, NY 10027

Copyright © 1988 by Teachers College, Columbia University

Illustrations by Daniel Ransom.

Library of Congress Cataloging-in-Publication Data

Althouse, Rosemary, 1932–
    Investigating science with young children/Rosemary Althouse.
       p.   cm.
    Bibliography: p.
    ISBN 0-8077-2912-4 (pbk.)
    1. Science—Study and teaching (Preschool)   I. Title.
LB1140.5.S35A46   1988   88–19990
372.3'5044—dc19   CIP

ISBN: 0-8077-2912-4

Manufactured in the United States of America

99   98   97   7   6

This book is dedicated to my young friends—
Alec, Matthew, John, Sara, Becky, and Wesley.

CONTENTS

PREFACE

Teaching science by a process approach is an exciting adventure for both teachers and children. There is neither a predetermined sequence of events for children nor a specific set of directions for the teacher. Process science is an open-ended approach, and the direction learning will take is determined, for the most part, by the children. This method requires that teachers understand how children learn, know the possibilities a topic offers for active learning, be familiar with suitable materials, and know how to use effective guidance techniques.

It is not enough to read about process science; you must use it to find out how much children enjoy and learn from this method. This book represents my experiences and those of several nursery school and kindergarten teachers who have successfully used process science with three-, four-, and five-year-old children. (Throughout, the specific ages of children have been underlined for your reference.) In Part I, I discuss the background information necessary to understand and appreciate the process approach to science. A reference list is included at the end of this first part. Part II, the major portion of the book, presents 85 activities you can use to guide children in exploring science. The activities in each chapter are presented in sequential order. This does not mean, however, that you must follow the exact sequence of activities. The interests and abilities of the group of children you are teaching will determine the direction learning will take. Try process science and find out how eager children are to learn when they are actively involved in their own learning.

ACKNOWLEDGMENTS

I wish to thank Winthrop College, the School of Education, and the Macfeat Early Childhood Laboratory School and its teachers Lori Jones, Mary Rix, and Mary Watson for testing my ideas. I am indebted to Susan Ghent, kindergarten teacher, Great Falls Elementary School, Great Falls, South Carolina, for testing my ideas and for many of the photographs that illustrate this book. I also want to thank Jim Linder, principal, Great Falls Elementary School, and Nancy Gates, supervisor, early childhood education, Chester County School, Chester, South Carolina, for making it possible for me to work with Ms. Ghent. I am grateful to Jean Morse for her patience and understanding during the typing of the manuscript.

PART I

Understanding the Process Approach

Teachers of young children teach science throughout the school day often without knowing it. Mixing paints, playing with water, building with blocks, digging holes, and making snacks are daily activities encountered in most programs. These self-paced activities may be defined as science experiences. Why are these science experiences, while others such as listening to stories, resting on mats, and celebrating birthdays are not? What is science? If teachers already teach science, how can science instruction be improved so that children receive optimal benefits from their experiences? The discussions about science in this part of the book are intended to answer the above questions.

Science may be defined as both product and process. It is a body of useful and practical knowledge—product—and a way of finding out about the environment—process. Williams (1985) states, "Science is not only the knowledge we acquire and have acquired from our study, but it is also the process or the way we study our physical world and the attitude we develop toward our world" (p. 8). The emphasis on teaching science to young children should be on *process,* or how to learn, rather than on *product,* or what to learn.

Science, unfortunately, is often taught to young children through demonstrations and lectures in the form of facts, concepts, and generalizations rather than through active child interaction and exploration. This product approach to science may be contrasted with a process approach by describing two classrooms as follows.

CLASSROOM I

Children are seated in a circle in front of their teacher as she demonstrates how to make green paint. At an easel she paints a yellow circle and then covers it with a blue circle. The paints mix to make green, and the teacher asks, "What colors did I use to make green paint?" The correct answers are reinforced by the teacher who says, "That's right. Good! Yes, yellow and blue make green." Other secondary colors are mixed from the primary colors, and children are asked questions about the color changes. Next the teacher reads *Color Kittens,* a book about mixing colors, to reinforce the concepts taught.

CLASSROOM II

The teacher places blue and yellow paints at an easel, and the children use these colors to paint. They soon discover a third color, green. A child says to the teacher, "Look at my paper. I made green." The teacher responds by asking, "Can you make green again?" The child makes several shades of green, each time naming the color by exclaiming, "I made green." Other children begin mixing paints to make green. Experimentation continues for several days as the children explore various shades of green with tempera paints. They begin to look for similarities and to make comparisons. They are overheard saying: "I made green too." "My green looks like your green." "My green is darker than your green." "My green is lighter than your green." The teacher asks: "Can you find the lightest green? Can you find the darkest green? Where does this green belong?" The teacher encourages the children to place the greens in a sequence from lightest to darkest.

The teacher in the first classroom is using a product approach to teaching science, and the teacher in the second classroom is using a process approach. Emphasis in the first classroom is on memorizing facts and concepts about color. Here the children are passive learners as they observe the teacher mixing colors and listen to her explanations about color. There is no opportunity for the children to learn through direct experience.

In the second classroom, children are actively engaged in their own learning. The teacher encourages active learning by asking open-ended questions, making encouraging comments, and showing an interest in and enthusiasm for what children are doing. Children learn about the physical properties of color as they explore and make discoveries. They observe and classify colors as light or dark green. They predict what will happen when more or less blue or yellow paint is added to the original color. These children behave, in an elementary way, like scientists in a laboratory.

It is through action on objects and first-hand experiences that children learn about their world. Teachers who understand how children learn are facilitators of learning, not imparters of knowledge. Their first responsibility is to encourage children to think for themselves and to act on their own ideas.

THE THEORETICAL FRAMEWORK

A process approach is recommended for teaching science to young children because it allows them to learn in a manner compatible with their cognitive development. Smith (1987) states, "A theoretical framework for a pre-school science curriculum integrates the child's construction of knowledge with science-related experiences and promotes active, child-initiated action on objects and observation changes" (p. 35). Children are motivated to act on their environment in order to learn to their satisfaction why something happens. As they explore their world, they engage, in a childlike way, in the processes of science.

CHILDREN'S COGNITIVE DEVELOPMENT

Since the early 1960s the work of the Swiss psychologist Jean Piaget has had a growing influence on the teaching of science to preschool, kindergarten, and elementary school children. According to Bybee and Sund (1982), Piaget explains children's intense curiosity and desire to act upon the environment by a self-regulatory process called equilibration. When something in the environment does not fit with what children already know, they find themselves in a state of confusion or mental imbalance—disequilibration. In order to return to a sate of satisfaction or mental balance—equilibration—they are motivated to act on their environment. Children may explore objects or ideas in such a way that what they find out can be fitted into their existing conceptual framework, a process termed assimilation. During assimilation if concepts are changed or new ones formed, the process of accommodation takes place. It is through the mental processes of assimilation and accommodation that learning occurs.

Children playing with a large magnet, for example, find that it will pick up many more paper clips than a smaller magnet. They respond by fitting "large magnet" into their already existing mental structures for big, powerful objects (assimilation). The teacher introduces a small but very strong magnet. The children find that the small magnet picks up more paper clips than the large magnet. This information does not fit in with their concept of small objects as weak and large objects as strong. They find themselves in a state of disequilibration. In order to assimilate this new information and return to a state of equilibration, they accommodate by creating a new structure for small but powerful magnets. Later, through many experiences with little but powerful objects, children begin to understand that not all big objects are powerful and not all little objects are weak. It is, therefore, through actions on objects that children encounter discrepencies in their environment and are motivated to find answers that satisfy them. In this way children structure their own knowledge. Piaget (1970) states, "The essential functions of intelligence consist in understanding and in inventing, in other words in building up structures by structuring reality" (p. 27).

Three types of knowledge

Piaget describes three types of knowledge acquired by children: physical knowledge, logico-mathematical knowledge, and social knowledge. *Physical knowledge* is the knowledge that children derive directly from objects. This includes information about properties of objects (shapes, odor, size) as well as how objects react to different actions on them (bounce, jump, roll). *Logico-mathematical knowledge* develops from physical knowledge as children create and invent relationships among objects (Piaget, 1970). Through experimentation with a rubber ball, children learn its physical properties. It bounces, floats in water, and falls down when thrown into the air. The children in Classroom II discovered that blue and yellow paint mixed together made green paint. This discovery was dependent upon the properties of the paints and the children's actions on them.

Logico-mathematical knowledge develops when children place a ball with other balls, count the number of balls, rearrange them several times, and find that each time the number of balls remains the same. This relationship does not depend on the properties of the balls, but rather on the relationships children created among them. In Classroom II the children created the relationship between light and dark green as they put the colors in order from lightest to darkest.

Social knowledge is different from physical and logico-mathematical knowledge since children gain social knowledge from their culture and their interactions with people. The fact that chairs are made to sit on, that a certain color is called green, and that July 4th is our nation's birthday are a part of our culture. This kind of knowledge is transmitted from one generation to another. Social knowledge can be valuable in motivating children to act on objects or ideas. In Classroom II children were motivated to continue mixing yellow and blue paint when they observed other classmates making lighter and darker shades of green.

Although the types of knowledge differ from one another, they are interrelated in the young child's thinking. Children must have a logico-mathematical framework in which to acquire knowledge about physical objects, and they must have physical objects to construct logico-mathematical knowledge (Kamii, 1985). In the example of mixing paints, children could not construct the relationships lighter green and darker green if they could not distinguish color properties of objects (physical knowledge). Likewise, children could not describe the colors as lighter or darker if they could not put them into some kind of relationship (logico-mathematical knowledge). The word used by children to name the color "green" is an example of social knowledge. Each language has its own word for identifying a color.

SCIENCE PROCESSES FOR YOUNG CHILDREN

In order to learn about the world in which they live, children must be given opportunities to discover the physical properties of objects and, by acting on them, to construct meaningful relationships between and among them. Piaget (1970) states "knowledge is derived from action. . . . To know an object is to act upon it and to transform it" (p. 29). A process approach to teaching science makes possible physical encounters with objects and the discovery of relationships among them. As children act on objects, they

5

use the processes of science that relate to all science disciplines. McNairy (1985) states:

> Of the eleven scientific processes identified by the American Association for the Advancement of Science, several can be experienced, at a primitive level, by young children and can provide opportunities for basic skills development. . . . Among the basic processes that are appropriate for young children are observation, classification, measurement, computation, experimentation, and prediction. (p. 385)

Science—A Process Approach (SAPA), a K–6 program of the American Association for the Advancement of Science, includes for K–3 the following processes: observing, classifying, inferring, predicting, using numbers, communicating, measuring, and using space/time relationships (Commission on Science Education, 1972).

In the following sections, I will discuss ten science processes in terms of young children. My selection includes four of the six processes identified by McNairy and SAPA—observing, classifying, measuring, and predicting—and four processes identified only by SAPA—making inferences, communicating, using numbers, and using space/time relationships. I am also including drawing conclusions, because young children often give explanations for why something happens. Children's explanations are not always accurate and are subject to change. They are, however, valid since they are based on children's interpretations of what they observe. Making comparisons is included since children compare objects as they experiment and often place them in some kind of relationship. Making comparisons is the first step in seriation. By choosing these ten processes, I do not intend to suggest that young children do not use other processes or that all of the processes identified are consistently used by young children. These are the processes that, for the most part, have been identified by science educators and, in my experience, children use as they act on objects.

Observing

Anyone who has worked with young children knows that they observe constantly. Kamii and DeVries (1978) describe two kinds of physical knowledge activities that demonstrate the importance of observation. In the first kind of activity, involving the movement of objects, children's actions are primary and their observations secondary. Throwing a ball at a target is an example of this kind of activity. The action is primary because there is an observable relationship between throwing the ball and hitting the target. A child can change the direction of the ball and determine where it hits the target. In the second kind of activity, involving changes in objects, children's observations are primary and their actions are secondary. Mixing paints is an example of this kind of activity. A child observes color changes as he or she mixes paints. The changes in the paint's color depends more on the properties of the paints than on the actions of the child. There is another kind of activity that falls somewhere between movement and change. Floating objects, playing with magnets, and looking through a magnifying glass are examples of activities that fall into this category. In these kinds of activities changes and movements in objects are primarily the result of the properties of objects. Although Kamii and DeVries do not recommend the third type of activity, they mention that many are found in early childhood texts under the heading of science.

Unfortunately teachers often decide what children should learn and attempt to teach it through verbalization and demonstration. You should introduce activities to children that involve them as active learners who act on objects and observe the results of their actions.

Classifying

Classification is the process of putting objects, people, or events into groups or categories based on their similarities. Classification opportunities can evolve out of children's classroom experiences. Two kindergarten children were talking about a group of model dinosaurs. One said, "Let's put all the green dinosaurs together and all the red dinosaurs together." The other child said, "O.K. Then, let's put all the man-eating dinosaurs together and all the plant-eating dinosaurs together." These children were allowed to invent their own classification systems based upon their knowledge of dinosaurs.

Classification involves logico-mathematical knowledge since children create the relationships between and among objects. Physical knowledge is necessary since children must know the properties of objects in order to place them, physically or mentally, into groups.

Comparing

When children become familiar with the attributes of objects, they begin to make comparisons between and among them. This ability to make comparisons leads to seriation, the arrangement of objects, events, or people into a series along some criterion such as size, length, number, and so forth. These relationships should evolve from children's real experiences in the classroom. A five-year-old was mixing food coloring in baby food jars filled with water. She made two reds and compared them. She said, pointing to the jars, "This is red. This is kinda red." Her teacher encouraged her to make other "reds" and compare them. The various shades were placed in five jars, and the jars were arranged in order from the lightest to the darkest red.

Children often experiment with materials and place them in some kind of relationship. This relationship is logico-mathematical and must be determined by the children themselves.

Communicating Children often share their findings with teachers and classmates. A kindergarten teacher placed flashlight batteries and bulbs and insulated wire on the science table. She asked, "Can you make the light burn?" Several children found various ways to light the bulb. The children showed and described their arrangements. As a result children who had not approached the science table began to experiment with batteries, bulbs, and wires to create their own arrangements. The teacher encouraged the children to draw pictures of their arrangements. She put the pictures in a book, which the children entitled, "How to Make a Light Burn."

Children do not always disclose their discoveries through verbalization. They may communicate how they are thinking about a problem through their behavior. It is important for you to observe children to discover how they solve problems by acting on objects.

During water play a four-year-old girl poured water into a wide funnel placed in a narrow, transparent container. Her attention was centered on the water going out of the funnel rather than on the water level in the container. Her concentration did not shift from the funnel to the container until the water overflowed and wet the floor. She immediately emptied the container and began the same process again. After a second accident, she found a large container that allowed her to view the water level. If the teacher had not observed the entire episode, she would never have known the child had a problem nor observed her strategy for solving it. It was not until after the child had solved her own problem that the teacher asked, "Jane, why did you choose a larger container?"

Inferring

Based on information gathered through observation and experimentation, children begin to make inferences or "educated guesses" about happenings in their environment. The logic of children's inferences is based upon their powers of observation and physical encounters with their environment.

You can help children make logical inferences by encouraging them to examine different aspects of a situation. Four- and five-year-old children were given powdered sugar, a sugar cube, and granulated sugar to explore. After using all their senses to investigate the materials, the children decided that the cubes of sugar and the granulated sugar were the same. They insisted, however, that the powdered sugar was flour flavored with sugar. Later flour was introduced, and the children found it did not dissolve in water like powdered sugar. They put sugar in the flour and compared it with the powdered sugar. No matter how much or how little sugar was added to the flour, it did not taste the same as the powdered sugar.

The teacher brought an electric blender to class and allowed the children to grind granulated sugar in it. Then the children examined the sugar and decided that it looked, tasted, and reacted in water like the powdered sugar. Most of the children decided that the powdered sugar was indeed a form of sugar, while a few were still undecided. The children's ability to make accurate inferences was dependent upon the various experiences provided by the teacher.

Concluding

During experimentation children arrive at various explanations to explain the information they receive. In a kindergarten, one child planted a bean seed in a cup of sand. He put the cup on a window sill and watered the seed each day for two weeks. The expected bean plant did not appear. The child told his teacher, "My bean didn't grow. That sand is no good." He selected one variable as the explanation for the bean's failure to grow. He didn't consider other variables such as the bean seed itself, the amount of water put on the seed each day, the temperature, or light. One bean-seed experiment is not sufficient to determine whether or not bean seeds will sprout in sand.

In contrast, several five-year-old children found little oak trees under an oak tree growing on their playground. They dug them up and discovered that each oak tree was

9

growing from an acorn. The children gathered acorns and soil samples from under the tree. They took the acorns inside and planted them in jars containing the soil. Some children watered the containers each day; others watered them occasionally or forgot to water them at all. A few of the acorns sprouted, and this success motivated the children to plant other kinds of seeds. The teacher supplied bean and corn seeds, the children brought seeds from home, and other seeds were found on the playground. Pots and jars were labeled with the kind of seed and name of the child who planted it. In addition, leaves, rocks, and sticks were planted in hope that new plants would grow from them. The children recorded the growth of the plants in drawings or dictated their findings to the teacher. After many discussions about their data, the children concluded that plants grow from seeds but not from leaves, sticks, or stones.

The conclusions the children made from the results of these experiments were *true for them* based upon their experiences with seeds and their stage of development. You should strive to give children additional time and materials to explore their environment to the fullest until all avenues of discovery open to them are exhausted. Without sufficient time to explore, children cannot acquire the necessary physical knowledge to help them think logically.

Predicting

Children make predictions as they explore and experiment with materials: "It will float if you put it in water." "Don't bring the snow inside. It will melt." "It's raining and the ground will be wet. We won't be able to go outside." The accuracy of their predictions are determined by their past experiences and how accurately they interpret their environment.

A group of three-year-olds were playing with a balance and a variety of shells. Some of the children did not realize that when one pan was lower than the other, the shell in the lower pan was heavier. The teacher encouraged the children to hold a shell in each hand and decide which shell was heavier. Then the shells were placed in the balance pan. The children noticed that the pan with the heavier shell was lower than the pan with the lighter shell. They began to understand that with the balance they could compare objects and discover the heavier one. The

10

teacher introduced shells that varied only slightly in weight. The children were surprised when their predictions about the shells were sometimes incorrect. The teacher had introduced a discrepancy in their environment. They could no longer depend solely on their sight and kinesthetic sense to guide them. The children learned that more information was needed before predictions could be made with accuracy.

You can encourage children to make predictions by asking thought provoking questions such as

What happened?
Why do you think it happened?
What do you think will happen next?

The more information they have, the better guesses children can make.

Using numbers

There are opportunities for children to use one-to-one correspondence and enumeration during their explorations of objects and events. Situations arise such as each clay pot needs a label; a straw is needed for each child; a ball knocked down four blocks; or my bubble is bigger than yours.

Several five-year-old children were helping their teacher make ice cream. The teacher asked, "How will we know when we have put seven cups of milk in the ice cream?" A child said, "I know. I'll put a mark on a piece of paper every time you pour a cup of milk." As each cup of milk was poured and counted, a line was drawn on the paper. Both enumeration and one-to-one correspondence were involved in this experience.

A group of three- and four-year-old children were blowing bubbles in the playground. They described their bubbles as big, little, and middle-sized. As they saw the bubbles go into the air, the children counted them. Although their ability to enumerate was limited, they began to assign a number name to each bubble. It is almost impossible to teach science without using numbers in some way.

Measuring

Children's measurements should be approximations rather than exact units. A child may show the height of his corn plant by drawing a picture, using a strip of paper, or indicating "how tall" with his hands.

Several five-year-olds kept a record of the growth of their bean and corn plants. Each time a change occurred in the growth of the plants, the children drew pictures to record the changes. Although the pictures were not the same as photographs, they revealed growth by showing the addition of plant parts and the increase in the size of the plants over a period of time.

Using strips of adding machine paper, a teacher helped children measure their heights and the length of their arms, legs, hands, and feet. The children pasted the various strips of paper on large pieces of construction paper. They noticed that certain parts of their bodies were longer than others and that some were approximately the same length. Exploring the lengths of body parts continued by measuring fingers, toes, and faces. Later the children measured "how big" they were around the neck, arm, leg, and wrist. Parts were compared by the children using terms such as "big," "bigger," "biggest"; "long," "longer," "longest"; and "longer than" and "bigger than."

Using space/time relations

Children construct space/time relations as they explore their environment. Space/time relationships are created when children stack blocks to keep them from falling, plant a seed and watch it grow, throw balls at a moving target, draw pictures to show what they do at school, and crawl through boxes.

A kindergarten teacher assembled an obstacle course on the children's playground. Directional terms, such as "up," "down," "over," and "under," were used by the teacher as the children moved through space. Children were overheard describing their movements as follows: "I'm walking on top of the footprints." "Let's climb over the box." "It's not far to the end of the ladder." "We went under the box." "I ran across the balance beam."

Nursery school children often have difficulty remembering the sequence of daily events. "What time do we — ——?" is a familiar question. One teacher took photographs of the children arriving in the morning, playing in the classroom, eating snacks, and leaving to go home. He discussed each picture with the children. Then he asked the children: "Which photograph shows what you do when you come to school in the morning? Which photograph shows what you do before snack? After snack? When it's time to go home?" The children helped the teacher put the photographs in sequential order. Then the children referred to the photographs when they wanted to know, "What happens next?"

CONCLUSIONS

Engaged in the above processes of science, children develop physical and logico-mathematical knowledge. As a teacher, if you are to guide children effectively, you must be aware of how children structure their knowledge and how they use the science processes as they explore their world. You must not impose your thoughts on children or give them the idea that there are *predetermined right* answers to their questions. You must allow children to formulate their own explanations for what they find. You can be a successful science teacher, if you encourage children to act on objects and to continue their actions until they are fully satisfied with the outcome.

THE ROLE OF THE TEACHER

Perhaps the most crucial factor in teaching science to young children is the teacher's attitude toward science. In my experience, I have found two prevalent ideas that prevent teachers from becoming successful science teachers. The first is, "I don't know anything about science," and the second is, "Young children can't learn science."

A misinterpretation of what science involves and unpleasant memories of science experiences in the elementary grades stop many teachers from attempting to teach science. From their experiences teachers concluded that science came from books, had to be memorized, and favored the smartest students. Unfortunately, many teacher education institutions do not prepare their students to teach science to preschool and kindergarten children. As an early childhood teacher, therefore, you may have little or no formal preparation for teaching science. What is important to understand is that young children learn best through activity and that a process approach to teaching science is compatible with the way young children grow and develop.

OBTAINING BACKGROUND INFORMATION

Books and articles

Where can you obtain more information on teaching science? There are a few good books offering a theoretical background and many practical suggestions for teaching science to young children, as well as articles describing the relationship between how children learn and the teaching of science. Some of these books and articles are included in the list of references at the end of Part I of this book.

Professional organizations

Your membership in professional organizations such as the National Association for the Education of Young Children, the Association for Childhood Education International, the National Science Teachers Association, and regional and state early childhood associations provide opportunities to attend conferences and institutes specially designed for teachers of young children. The periodicals published by such organizations—*Young Children, Childhood Education, Science and Children,* and *Dimensions*—are excellent and give you up-to-date information about how children learn and how this knowledge may be used in planning all phases of the curriculum, including science. Sharing ideas with other teachers and talking with curriculum specialists are other ways you can obtain information.

Science texts   Teachers are often afraid that they do not know enough science content to teach science. One of the best ways to learn more about science is to read through an elementary science textbook series and to consult encyclopedias and children's science books written and edited by scientists. Familiarity with content will help you develop appropriate science activities for children.

SELECTING APPROPRIATE ACTIVITIES

Action   You should plan activities that permit young children to *act* on objects and to *observe* the results of their actions on objects. An activity such as throwing a ball at a target is appropriate since the child knows at once whether or not the ball reached the target.

Copple, Sigel, and Saunders (1979) state the following basic principles that should guide the selection of activities and materials:

1. Choose activities that allow the child to be the cause of the action and employ a "hands on" approach.
2. Choose activities and materials that allow teachers to employ inquiry strategies that focus attention on discrepancies and on the *actions* in the situation.
3. Choose activities that help the child focus on the transformations, on change from one state to another, rather than on the beginning and the end states.

Different science problems and experiences have different educational value in providing the child with a meaningful experience. For example, asking children to make astronomical observations and then report them would be beyond their competence. Problems such as how we digest our food, or how nutrition helps us grow are relatively ineffective in promoting scientific investigation because they involve nonobservable changes or long-range outcomes. In either event children cannot directly observe the transformation. Young children gain little from such problems. Taking these considerations into account leads to another important guideline:

4. Select problems where the rate of change is rapid and observable, such as water changing color or ice melting. (p. 125)

Science processes

In addition to meeting the above criteria, the activities you select should promote the development of the science processes described in the previous chapter. Through a process approach to science, children can develop these processes as they explore both objects and ideas. You will recall that they use the information obtained from their actions on objects—physical knowledge—to invent and create new relationships between and among objects—logico-mathematical knowledge.

DESIGNING THE CLASSROOM ENVIRONMENT

Science center

A science center is a must in the classroom. If space is at a premium in your room, the center does not have to be large or elaborate. A small area can be designated where children can find and bring materials of interest to them. One of the best science centers I have seen was an upright, painted orange crate placed in a Head Start room. It held an equal arm balance, a number of large magnifying glasses, color paddles, and a variety of sea shells.

You should change a science center as the interests and abilities of children change. A teacher observed four-year-old children playing for several days with a large horseshoe magnet and several bar magnets. They were fascinated by the interactions of the magnets. In order to encourage further interest and experimentation, the teacher added round and cylindrical shaped magnets. It was not long until the children were building constructions with the magnets and describing what was happening to them as "sticking together," "having power," and "jumping away."

Materials

Although the science center is often the hub of science activities, any area of your room may become a science learning center. Materials such as blocks, wheel toys, a water table, and a work bench encourage science explorations. You can utilize any learning center in teaching science to young children.

A teacher placed round and flat objects on the science table. The children began experimentation at once and soon discovered that some of the objects rolled. This discovery led to a search in the classroom for other objects that rolled. The children soon found beads, crayons, rhythm sticks, pencils, and wheel toys. Soon the activities that began at the science center involved experimentation with rolling objects in every center of the room.

A variety of materials should be available for active exploration. These materials do not have to be expensive or specialized. McNairy (1985) states:

> Learning in the context of sciencing requires materials that are normally found in early childhood classrooms: various sizes and shapes of blocks, cars, trucks, housekeeping equipment, art, sand, water, work tools, and manipulative materials and equipment. It is necessary, however, that these materials be placed so that children have access to them at all times. (p. 390)

You should explore the possibilities of the materials you are planning to introduce to children. Through manipulating materials, you may discover properties of objects previously unknown to you. One teacher was surprised when she discovered that a drop of water could magnify a small object. Her discovery opened up new possibilities for exploring magnification with children.

Safety must always come first in the classroom. Hitting rocks without goggles, playing with loose iron filings, and handling sharp objects are examples of activities that have no place in a science program for young children.

INTRODUCING MATERIALS

Present Kamii and DeVries (1978) suggest several ways to introduce materials to children. The first is simply to put out materials and wait for the children to gravitate to them. Children respond spontaneously to high-interest materials such as balances, blocks, and balls. A teacher placed sea shells on the science table, and several children immediately hurried to explore the shells. Comments such as "Mine is bigger than yours," "I found a little one," and

"My shell is bigger than any of them" were overheard by the teacher. He placed an equal arm balance on the science table and experimentation with the shells began immediately.

Invite action

A second way you can introduce materials is to put out familiar objects and ask, "What can you do with these materials?" A kindergarten teacher placed objects that rolled and did not roll on the science table. Some children looked at the materials but made no attempt to manipulate them. The teacher said, "See what you can do with these objects." Interaction with the objects began at once. Explorations varied from building with the objects to attempts to roll them. The teacher posed questions, made comments, and added new materials to stimulate further explorations.

Ask a question

A third way for you to begin an activity is to pose a question. One teacher provided children with a soap solution in a shallow container and several straws. He asked, "Can you use a straw to blow bubbles?" The children's responses were immediate. Later small juice cans with tops and bottoms removed were added and experimentation continued.

Use children's questions

A fourth way you can introduce an activity is to utilize questions posed by children. A five-year-old child examined a pumpkin plant growing in the classroom. He accidentally broke off part of the plant and told his teacher, "I didn't mean to break the pumpkin plant. Can I put it in water and grow a new plant?" The teacher said, "Try it and find out." She wondered if each day the child would remember to put water in the jar with the pumpkin slip. He did remember the water, and a few days later he brought the jar to the teacher and said, "Look, my plant has roots." His activity interested other children in the class, and they began a series of explorations with plants.

ENCOURAGING STUDENT EXPLORATION

Guiding children as they interact with materials is probably the most important and the most difficult aspect of science teaching. Knowing when to intervene with a question or a suggestion and when to say nothing is an acquired art.

Observe

You must be a careful observer of children to make educated guesses about how and what they are thinking about a problem. A child's *actions* often give you a clue. Four-year-old John was attempting to build a high building with large blocks ignoring the small blocks at the base that made the building unstable. The teacher asked, "John, why do you think your building keeps falling?" John said, "I don't know." The building fell again, and John looked at the teacher with a puzzled look. She asked him, "What do you think would happen if you chose a different block for the base? Why don't you try a larger block this time?" John chose a large block for the base, and his building remained standing. The teacher asked, "John, how did you keep it from falling?" "Look," he said pointing to the base, "I used big blocks at the bottom."

Model behavior

To encourage experimentation, it may be necessary for you to model behavior for children. A group of four-year-old children placed several round objects on a tile floor. They blew hard on the objects, and several of them moved across the floor. Although the children experimented with various ways to move objects on the tile floor, they did not think of putting objects on the rug. After several days of experimentation, the teacher asked, "What would happen if you put a bead on the rug?" The children ignored his question and continued their explorations. Later the teacher placed a bead on the rug and blew on it. The bead didn't move, and the teacher said, "The bead won't move." This activity interested the children, who told the teacher, "We can make it move." They began experimenting with several objects on the rug. Later they tried moving objects on table tops and in water. The teacher's behavior suggested to the children new ways to explore objects.

Make-believe play

You can expect children to engage in make-believe play as they explore objects. The pretend play of young children will be more fanciful than that of older children. A three-year-old child moved a feather by blowing through a straw and pretended the feather was a bird. She said, "I can make my bird fly." Two five-year-old children pretended that the bubbles they made were spaceships. They chased them saying, "Look how high our spaceships are going."

Make-believe play often involves solving problems.

The child who pretended a feather was a bird wanted her "bird" to "fly" across the table. She blew too hard into the straw and the bird "flew" off the table. She continued to blow into the straw until she succeeded in moving the "bird" across the table. The boys playing with the "bubble spaceships" wanted their spaceships to go over the school building. They found through experimentation that blowing into the wind had a very different effect on their "spaceships" from blowing with their backs to the wind.

As a teacher, it is your responsibility to help children focus their attention on their actions on objects and the results of their actions. A five-year-old child built a house with several large boxes. The teacher asked, "How do you know where your rooms are?" The child indicated the location of the rooms by pointing and naming several unoccupied spaces. The teacher asked, "How would you use the boxes to divide the rooms?" As a result of the teacher's question, the little girl decided to use additional boxes to make rooms. She said, "I won't need as many boxes for the bathroom. I'm making it the littlest room."

Animism and artificialism

Children's explanations for why something happens often reveal their beliefs in animism—inanimate objects are alive and have human characteristics—and in artificialism—human beings create natural phenomena. A five-year-old child's explanation for why a plastic egg moved across a water table was "It wanted to move." Closer observation and further experimentation resulted in a different explanation. The child said, "I made the egg move when I made waves in the water with my hands." While planting seeds a three-year-old child said, "My daddy will make them grow." He decided not to water the seeds and lost interest in caring for them. Later he observed the other children's seeds sprout and listened to their discussions about growing seeds. He learned that seeds needed water to grow and decided to plant seeds again. This time with the help of the teacher he watered his seeds every day. As children grow and have more experiences, the belief in animism and artificialism decreases and children's thinking becomes more logical.

Sharing views

You should encourage children to interact with each other and to exchange viewpoints. In a kindergarten there were several cylindrical, transparent containers at the water table. Some were filled with water and others were empty. Jack dropped a block into one filled with water. "Look," he said, "the block looks bigger." Gary said, "You made it grow bigger." Jack took the block out of the water and showed it to Gary who said, "O.K. Let's put the block into another jar of water." The boys tested the block in several jars filled with water. The block looked larger in each of the jars. When the block was removed from the jars, it no longer appeared to be larger. The children agreed that the actual size of the block did not change.

The teacher had observed the children's experimentation and overheard their comments. She moved to the water table and asked, "Why do you think the block looks bigger in the jars?" "We don't know," said Gary. The teacher suggested, "Let's put the block into other containers of water." The teacher found round and square containers and gave them to the boys. Soon several children joined Gary and Jack. They noticed that the size of the block did not change in every container. The teacher asked, "Why do you think the block looks larger in some containers and not in others?"

The children began a discussion among themselves, and the teacher left them to solve their problem. From time to time she could hear them arguing, each giving his or her explanation for the strange phenomenon. Later she joined the children who told her, "The block looks bigger in round containers." One child said, "It's like our magnifying glasses." These children had shared opposing viewpoints and had come to a satisfactory conclusion.

CONCLUSIONS

If teachers are to be successful science teachers, they must be curious and investigative people. They must have the same love of learning that young children possess. Without it teachers will not communicate the spirit of inquiry to children. There are teachers who, unfortunately, feel that they must communicate knowledge to children. They do not *trust children to learn* through their own curiosity followed by their actions on objects. Elkind (1981) suggests that children abstract mediating structures from adult actions and that these structures may be necessary for academic success. In other words, an adult's enthusiasm for science and his or her investigative spirit can affect the child's acquisition of knowledge. Elkind states:

> Most good teachers are good mediators; that is really what good teaching means. But what are the characteristics of good teachers? They must, of course, know the subject matter and the children and try to present materials in ways that are interesting and non-stressful. But most important, good teachers must enjoy teaching and take pleasure in the materials they present to their students. (p. 23)

If you understand how children construct knowledge, adopt a process approach to teaching science, are well prepared, and possess curiosity and enthusiasm for learning, you can be a good teacher of science.

References

Bybee, R. W., & Sund, R. B. (1982). *Piaget for educators* (2nd ed.). Columbus, Ohio: Charles E. Merrill Publishing Co.

Commission on Science Education. (1972). *Science: A process approach, commentary for teachers.* New York: AAAS/Xerox Corporation.

Copple, C., Sigel, I., & Saunders, R. (1979). *Educating the young thinker: Classroom strategies for cognitive growth.* New York: D. Van Nostrand Co.

Elkind, D. (1981). How grown-ups help children learn. *Principal, 60*(5), 20–24.

Kamii, C. F. (1985). *Young children reinvent arithmetic.* New York: Teachers College Press.

Kamii, C., & DeVries, R. (1978). *Physical knowledge in preschool education: Implications of Piaget's theory.* New York: Prentice-Hall.

McNairy, M. R. (1985). Sciencing: Science education for early childhood. *School Science and Mathematics, 95*(5), 383–93.

Piaget, J. (1970). *Science of education and the psychology of the child.* New York: Grossman.

Smith, R. F. (1987). Theoretical framework for preschool science experiences. *Science and Children, 42*(2), 34–40.

Williams, D. L. (1985). On science for young children. In M. McIntyre (Ed.), *Early childhood and science* (pp. 7–9). Washington, D.C.: National Science Teachers Association.

PART II

Activities for Experiencing Science

Each chapter in this part takes up a different subject to be investigated by young children by means of five to eight activities. At the beginning of the chapter, a short introduction explains the science processes to be explored and the general materials needed. For each activity there is a list of specific materials to be used and suggestions on introducing the activity. As the activity progresses, questions and comments you can use to guide children are set off for easy reference. These are presented as suggestions only, and you should adapt them to the interests and abilities of your group of children. The science processes in which children are engaging are noted in the margin. I have also included extensive comments made by children as they were participating in the activities. They will give you an idea of the enthusiasm children have for these activities, and the various directions their learning takes as they explore materials.

EXPLORING WATER

Water is a readily available, inexpensive material that young children enjoy. Although children make discoveries through unorganized water play, more varied opportunities to learn about water are provided when you help them focus on specific aspects of water play. I have found that young children will remain at a water table for long periods of time when they are investigating a problem suggested by the teacher, a classmate, or a new discovery.

Science processes

A considerable amount of what children learn about water depends upon careful *observation*. Children observe the color, odor, feel, and taste of water. They explore water and observe the results of their actions. They become familiar with the characteristics of water and make *comparisons* between big and little containers, big and little holes, and dry and wet paper. Learning the characteristics of objects and making comparisons between and among objects is the first step in *classification* and *seriation*. Children use *space/time relations* when they estimate how far water must fall to make big and little splashes. Children use *number* as they count the cups of water it takes to fill a container. *Measurement* is used as children make comparisons between the various containers: "If we fill the big jar with water, there won't be enough left to fill the little jar. This pitcher will hold more water than the cup." *Predictions* are made as children guess what will happen to water poured through sieves and colanders, and how many large cups will fill a bowl. Based upon previous observations, children make *inferences* such as "A heavy object made the big splash," and "The water is warm because it is in the sun." Children draw *conclusions* such as "Water comes out of big holes faster," and "Water makes paper towels wet." Children's conclusions are accurate because they are based upon their interpretations of what they observe.

Opportunities for *communication* occur as children talk with each other and the teacher about their discoveries. Older children may want to dictate their findings for the teacher to record, while younger children may insist on, "Watch, I'll show you what I did."

What you need for water activities

Transparent water table (Transparent is preferred although most water tables have white or blue linings.) *or*

Large, transparent plastic container at least 15″ × 13″ × 7″ (Several smaller containers may be substituted.)

When commercial equipment is not available, materials for water play can consist of "found materials."

ACTIVITY 1
DESCRIBING WATER

What you need   Water table *or* large plastic container

How you begin   You can introduce water play by filling a water table or a large plastic container with water. Children will gravitate naturally to the container and begin to play in the water.

Observing and communicating   You can encourage *observation* during water play by asking questions such as

> What does the water look like?
> What color is water?
> What happens when you move your hands in the water?

Older children may *describe* water as "clear," "like the rain," or "the color you can see through." Younger children may say that water is "white," "gray," or "not like the beach." Children's descriptions of water should be accepted since this is how water looks to them. Additional experiences with water help children to describe its color, taste, and smell more accurately.

Children should drink water from the same faucet used to fill the water table. Encourage them to *talk about* how water tastes. Younger children's descriptions are usually more naive than those of older children. They may describe water as tasting "good," "like water," or "cold," while older children may say, "It tastes like nothing," "It hasn't anything in it to taste," or "I don't taste anything."

Several three- and four-year-old children said water smelled like "the beach," "fish," and "the ocean," while five-year-old children said, "You can't smell water," "It smells like the rain," "It smells like nothing because there's nothing in it," and "It smells like it doesn't have a smell to it."

Concluding   Most children describe water indoors as feeling "cold" and outdoors as "cool," "cold," or "warm" depending on the temperature. One group of children suggested putting the classroom thermometer in the water. They observed the red line go down and up as they put the thermometer in and out of the water. They *concluded* that the temperature of the water was cooler than the temperature in their room.

Communicating and classifying

Encourage children to use their hands and arms in water play. You can ask,

> How does the water feel?
> What happens when you move your hands in the water?
> What happens when you take your hands out of the water?

One child said the water did not feel gritty since "there is no salt in it." As one group of children took their hands out of the water, they noticed the water droplets on the ends of their fingers. One child described the droplets as "beads on my fingers" and another as "rain on the ends of my fingers." Children may notice that if they lift their hands straight up, water runs down their arms. In one classroom black children thought the water had changed color and remarked, "The water is brown," while white children described the water as "white and shiny." Children can learn that water appears to change color depending on the color of its container. Each child will have his or her own way of describing the properties of water. As children *talk about* their experimentations, they begin to assign specific characteristics to water. Learning the attributes of a material is the first step in *classification*.

ACTIVITY 2
USING HANDS IN WATER

What you need   Water table *or* large plastic container

How you begin   Fill a water table or large plastic container with water. Encourage the children to vary their hand movements in the water. They may slap, push, hit, or pat the water. You can ask,

> What happens when you move your hands back and forth in the water? Slowly? Rapidly?
> Can you push the water away from you?
> What happens to the water when you hit it hard? Gently?

Communicating and using spatial relations   Some children will cup their hands, fill them with water, and lift them out of the water. Encourage children to *describe* what happens when they open their hands over the water. Children may say that the water "pops up," "jumps," "makes waves," or "makes a loud sound" when it hits the water in the water table. Children should cup water in their hands and release it at different distances from the water table. Simple *spatial* terms may be used such as "near," "high up," "low," "far from," and "close to." The sound of water and the amount of splashing will vary as the children drop water far above and close to the water table.

Observing   Children will *observe* that water runs through their fingers as they attempt to hold it in their hands. You can ask,

> Can you hold water in your hands?
> What happens to the water when you hold it?
> Can you hold the water in both hands?
> Does it help to hold the water if you cup your hands together?
> What happens to the water?

One child said, "I have holes in my fingers," and another, "I'm making it rain." When children move their hands rapidly in the water, they will notice that the "waves" move very fast, and when they move their hands slowly, the "waves" move slowly. Children will make different discoveries depending upon their background of experience, age, and above all, the skill of the teacher in asking questions.

ACTIVITY 3
DRYING HANDS ON PAPERS

What you need   Water table *or* large plastic container
Paper towels
Wax paper
Finger paint paper
Construction paper
Newsprint

How you begin   After children have been engaged in water play, offer them paper towels and wax paper to dry their hands and ask them to use both materials. Say to them,

> Are your hands dry?
> What does the paper look like?
> Why do you think the paper is wet?

Observing   Children will *notice* that the paper towels are wet, but their hands are dry. They may be surprised to see droplets of water on the wax paper. Comments made by one group of five-year-olds were "The paper is scratchy," "I want a real paper towel," and "This paper doesn't work. My hands are wet."

Concluding   When asked why there was water on the wax paper, the children answered, "The wax paper is hard," "Wax paper is for play dough," and "A paper towel dries better."

Comparing   Allow children to experiment with other kinds of paper such as finger paint paper, construction paper, and newsprint. Encourage the children to *compare* the papers by asking how they are different. Children will notice that some papers have water droplets and others soak up the water. Making comparisons is the first step in seriation.

ACTIVITY 4
EXPERIMENTING WITH CONTAINERS

What you need

Water table *or* large plastic container
Several transparent plastic containers of various sizes

How you begin

Put several clear, empty containers in the water and have the children fill the containers and pour water from one container to another.

Measuring

Encourage children to hold a container and pour water gradually into it. Ask questions to help children use *measurement* such as

Which container holds more water? Less water?
Which container is empty?
How does the container feel when it is empty? When it has a little water in it? When it is full of water?

Comparing

Children can place like containers or unlike containers in each hand and *compare* their weights when they are empty or filled with water. Containers may or may not feel alike depending upon the type of container and the amount of water in each container.

Using number and predicting

Ask questions to develop the use of *number* and the ability to make *predictions*:

How many cups did it take to fill the bottle?
How many jars do you think it will take to fill this container?

How investigation continues

With water and a supply of containers, children will devise their own activities. These may include filling containers until they overflow, comparing the amounts of water various containers will hold, pouring water from one container to another, pouring water from various distances and predicting how it will sound when it hits the water, filling containers with water and watching them sink, and pushing the mouth of empty containers down into the water and watching the containers come up. Children's explanations for what happens will vary. Some explanations that children have given are "Water causes my container to come back up," "Water makes things heavy," "This one is heavier because it's bigger," and "The water

30

makes a big splash 'cause I dropped it far up." Some children will experiment with containers and water for several days; others may be ready to move on to another activity in a few days. What children learn from their experimentations depends a great deal on the teacher's enthusiasm and interest shown in the children's discoveries.

USING FUNNELS, COLANDERS, AND STRAINERS

What you need   Water table *or* large plastic container
Several funnels
Several colanders
Several strainers

How you begin   Give children funnels, colanders, and strainers to use in their water play. Encourage them to fill these utensils with water.

Observing   Children may *notice* water coming out of a funnel, but they may not understand why water sometimes overflows when a funnel is used to fill a container. In her attempt to fill a bowl, a <u>four-year-old</u> kept pouring water in a funnel. She did not realize that the container was overflowing until it was too heavy for her to hold. She turned the funnel upside down and, surprised, said, "It has a hole."

Concluding   Suggest to the children that they fill a colander with water. The children may not realize that this is impossible because the colander has holes. In an effort to fill a colander with water, three children put two small pumpkins, several rocks, and a shell in a colander. They continued to pour water and were surprised when the water level in the colander did not rise. It wasn't until the next day that one of the children said, "We can't fill it; it has holes." Encourage further experimentation with colanders and strainers by asking questions such as

Can you fill the colander with water? Why not?
Where does the water go?
Can you fill the strainer with water?

Explanations given by one group of children for their difficulty in filling the utensils were "Because it has those square holes," "It's got all those holes," "It has big holes," and "It has too many holes." Allow children to experiment with the utensils until they are satisfied with their results.

ACTIVITY 6
WATCHING WATER FLOW

What you need   Water table *or* large plastic container
Large and small pencils
Styrofoam trays
Hammer
Large and small nails

How you begin   Using large and small pencils, punch holes in Styrofoam trays. Make large holes in some of the trays and small holes in others. Ask the children,

Can you fill the trays with water?

Some children may say, "No, it has holes," while others will try it out.

Predicting   Children will notice that the flow of water depends on the number and size of the holes. Encourage children to *predict* the amount of water that will come out of each tray. A teacher asked a group of five-year-olds, "What happens when you put water in the tray?" One child answered, "It goes out." The teacher asked, "Why?" and the child replied, "It has holes in it." The teacher asked, "Is the water coming out fast or slowly?" The child answered, "Fast, because the holes are big."

Concluding   Allow children to work at the workbench and hammer holes in trays with nails. From previous experiences with water, children can *predict* the kind of water flow they will get when water is poured into their trays. They probably will *conclude* that large holes are preferable to small holes when they want the water to flow steadily and quickly.

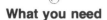

ACTIVITY 7
EXPERIMENTING WITH PLASTIC BAGS

What you need Water table *or* large plastic container
Zip Lock plastic bags
Nails *or* scissors
Paper bags

How you begin Put a hole in the bottom of several Zip Lock bags. Encourage children to fill the bags with water.

Observing One child who had never *described* the color of water held up a bag and said, "It looks like a mirror 'cause you can see through it." Another child said, "It's clear in the bag."

Concluding Children will squeeze the bags and watch the water come out of the holes. Some comments made by children were "It comes straight out," "The water won't stay in 'cause there is a hole in the bag," and "Is this bag busted? Water comes out."

Inferring Allow children to use nails or scissors and make as many large and small holes in the bags as they choose. Help the children to make *inferences* by asking questions such as

> Why do you think a lot of water is coming out of your bag?
> How many holes did you put in your bag?
> How big were the holes?
> Why are two streams of water coming out of your bag?

How investigation continues Encourage experimentation with other kinds of bags. Paper bags, for example, may introduce an element of surprise.

ACTIVITY 8
MAKING BUBBLES IN WATER

What you need

Water table *or* large plastic container
Paper towels
Sponges
Small rocks
Small transparent containers

When to use this activity

By now most children have noticed that some objects and the movements of their hands make bubbles in water. If children show an interest in bubbles earlier, this activity should be carried out at that time. One group of children put crumpled paper towels in the water and noticed bubbles around the towels. They immediately began experimenting with other materials and eventually made bubbles by moving their hands in water.

How you begin

You can introduce bubbles by asking children to observe a dry sponge placed in water. The children will notice bubbles rising to the top of the water. After watching the bubbles, allow children to play with other dry sponges. You can ask thought-provoking questions such as

> How did water get into the sponge?
> Why does water come out of the sponge? Show me how it comes out.
> How could you make more bubbles?

Some three- and four-year-old children's comments about sponges were as follows: "My momma scrubs with this. I got it wet." "There's water inside the sponge. I put it there." "My sponge has lots of water. It's heavy." "I can squeeze the sponge and make bubbles. You have to squeeze the sponge to make bubbles."

Inferring

Children will make *inferences* about the number and size of holes in the sponges. A five-year-old child said, "This sponge can make lots of bubbles 'cause the holes are big." Another one said, "I want the sponge with little holes to make little bubbles."

Observing

Encourage children to explore other safe and desirable materials. One group of children *watched* their teacher put

rocks in their aquarium. They were surprised when they saw bubbles around and above the rocks. It is sometimes better to test, one at a time, materials in small, transparent containers so that children can see the bubbles more distinctly.

THOUGHTS ON EXPLORING WATER

There are other water activities that you can initiate with children or that children may initiate themselves. The important thing is to give children opportunities to explore water and to guide them in their explorations.

MIXING COLORS

Color is a vital part of your children's lives. From birth to the time they enter nursery school, children have experienced color in many forms. Some children may have explored paints before their first school experience, but for many it is their introduction to painting. You can help children discover more about color by giving them the opportunity to mix paints. Children should be given the opportunity to make their own secondary colors, tints, and shades. Choose activities that allow paints to mingle freely and provide children with a variety of tools and materials. Not only will they discover new possibilities for the use of color in their art work, but they will be using the processes of science as well.

Science processes

Children must *observe* carefully to notice and remember the colors they mix to make new colors. Colors are *classified* according to their likenesses and differences, and seriation occurs when the relationships between and among colors are *compared*. Children make *predictions* about the colors they will make from mixing various paints and make *inferences* based upon the colors they obtain. *Space/time relations* are discovered as children use body parts to explore shapes and sizes. After many various experiences with paints, children draw *conclusions* about mixing colors: yellow and blue make green; blue and red make purple; red and yellow make orange; white makes colors lighter; black makes colors darker; red, yellow, and blue make brown (depending on the amount of each color). Children enjoy *describing* their pictures and talking in detail about how they painted them.

How the activities are organized

In activities 1–6, children mix the primary colors to make the secondary colors. In activities 7 and 8, white and black paint are introduced to encourage experimentation with making lighter and darker shades.

ACTIVITY 1
USING TEMPERA PAINT IN PRIMARY COLORS

What you need

Easel(s)
Paint carriers for painting at tables
Tempera paints—blue, yellow, and red
Brushes—1″, ¾″, and ½″ (long handles); ¼″ and ¹/₁₆″ (short handles)
Water jars
Newsprint
Jar lids

How you begin

Place blue and yellow tempera paint and a variety of brushes on the easel(s). Painting can also be done at a table with paints securely placed in paint carriers. Provide a jar of water at the easel or on the table for rinsing brushes. Observe children as they interact with the paints and brushes. Some children will explore paints for several days without calling attention to the green paint that results from mixing yellow and blue. Other children will inform their classmates and teachers as soon as the new color appears: "Look, I made green." "I made a new color." "What color is it?" "Watch me make green."

Observing

Help children *observe* what happens when they mix yellow and blue paint by making comments and asking questions such as

> How did you make green paint? Show me how you made green.
> That's a bright green. What colors did you mix to make that green?
> Can you mix yellow and blue again to make green?

Concluding

Give children many opportunities to mix blue and yellow paint and allow them to work at their own pace. After several days of experimentation, one five-year-old boy said, "I made two greens." The teacher asked, "Are they exactly alike?" "No," he replied, "but they're both green." "Yes," said the teacher, "this is light green, and that is dark green. How did you make light green?" "I don't know," he replied. Several weeks later the same child said, "I know how to make light green. Use a lot of yellow paint and a little blue paint."

Comparing   Encourage the development of seriation skills by asking children to *compare* the variations of color:

> Did you make light or dark green?
> How did you make light green? Dark green?
> Which green is lightest? Darkest?
> Can you put the greens in order from the lightest to the darkest?

How you continue   Place several jar lids on the easel(s) or at the table and encourage children to mix paints in the lids as well as directly on the paper. Experimentation with paints in jar tops usually results in wide variations of the same color.

Activities similar to those done to explore green paint may be used with children to discover orange. Place red and yellow tempera paint on the easel(s) or at a table. Observe children as they interact with the paints. Encourage children to mix the colors to make orange.

Communicating   When children begin to *talk about* mixing colors to make new colors, place red, blue, and yellow tempera paint on the easel(s). Children will soon mix the colors to discover purple, brown, and variations of other colors.

One three-year-old mixed red, blue, and yellow paint in jar tops for several days. When the teacher asked, "What color did you make?," Jim replied, "Brown." The teacher asked, "How did you make brown?" Jim replied, "I don't know." The teacher noticed that Jim continued to "make brown" in addition to other colors. She asked, "Jim, what colors did you mix to make brown?" He replied, "Red, yellow, and blue." After further experimentation, Jim could name the colors he had used to make brown. He was not aware, however, of the amount of each color he had used. This was not important at his stage of development. What was significant at the age of three was that he was aware that he could mix paints to make colors.

Five-year-old children will be able to *describe* how they make colors and variations of colors. One child said, "I made light green for the tree leaves and dark green for the grass. I used a wide brush to paint the grass and a narrow brush to make the tree leaves." Children should be offered a wide selection of brushes including both wide and narrow bristles and long and short handles. Children can select the brushes that are easiest for them to hold and manipulate and the widths they need to create the effects they want in their pictures.

39

ACTIVITY 2
USING FINGER PAINTS IN PRIMARY COLORS

What you need   Finger paint (commercial or homemade)—blue, yellow, and red
Finger paint paper

How you begin   At the same time children are mixing tempera paints, introduce blue and yellow finger paints. Children enjoy painting directly on formica tabletops or on finger paint paper. Ask the children:

> What color(s) do you want to use?
> Do you want blue? Yellow? Blue and yellow?

Eventually children will mix blue and yellow finger paint to make green.

Predicting   Children like to add paints in differing amounts to make variations in color. Encourage making *predictions* experimenting with blue and yellow paint. Ask questions such as

> What happens when you mix blue and yellow?
> What will happen if you add more blue paint? More yellow paint?
> What color will your hands be?
> Will they be the same color as the finger paint?
> Can you make part of your picture light green? Dark green?

Using spatial relations   Children can be encouraged to use different parts of their hands to finger paint. Different effects are obtained by painting with the fingertips, finger nails, palms, sides of the hand, back of the hand, and wrist. Help children become aware of *spatial relations* by exploring the various impressions made by their hands in the paint:

> What part of your hand made these marks?
> How did you make the lines go around your picture?
> How did you make the circles?
> These shapes touch each other. How did you make them?
> The little circle is inside the big circle. How did you make the little circle?
> Tell me about the shapes on your paper. What are they called?
> What part of your hand did you use to make the shapes?

One child said, "I made blue waves at the ocean. I put my thumb and pointer together. Then I moved my hand across the paper." And another child said, "I used my hands to make a green picture. Then I drew a square and made a smiling face inside the square with my finger nail."

How you continue   Introduce yellow and red finger paint, and plan activities similar to those used to mix yellow and blue finger paint. Later add blue finger paint to the red and yellow finger paint. Children will discover that they can make brown finger paint by mixing red, yellow, and blue. You can ask questions such as

> How did you make brown?
> Did you make brown with the tempera paints?
> What colors did you use?
> Can you make brown again?

Communicating   Four- and five-year-old children may describe brown as "reddish brown," "dark brown," "light brown," or "purplish brown." Encourage children to *talk about* the colors they mixed to get a specific color:

> Can you make reddish brown again?
> Did you use more red, blue, or yellow paint?
> What would happen if you used more blue paint? More yellow? More red?

ACTIVITY 3
BLOW PAINTING WITH PRIMARY COLORS

What you need

Tempera paints—blue, yellow, and red
Newsprint *or* manila drawing paper
Cardboard
Jumbo straws—several per child
Medicine droppers
Spoons

How you begin

Give children blue, yellow, and red liquid tempera paints, newsprint or manila drawing paper, jumbo straws, and three medium droppers. Tell the children to use the medicine droppers to put paint on the paper. Then have them blow through the straws and watch what happens to the paints. Children learn to vary how hard they blow and the direction they blow in order to create the desired effects.

Observing

Colors combine to make secondary colors and variations of colors. Help children *observe* the colors as they come together by asking questions and making comments such as

> What colors made orange?
> Watch the yellow and blue paint. What color will they make?
> I see the paints running together. What colors do you think they will make?

Predicting

Encourage children to *predict* the results of blow painting by asking them questions:

> What colors can you make with the blue and yellow paint?
> What will happen if you blow the yellow paint in this direction?
> What will happen if the red, yellow, and blue paint come together?

How investigation continues

Children can change the direction of the paints by moving their straws or by turning their papers. Paints can be dropped on cardboard with a medicine dropper or a spoon. Children can hold the cardboard and move it so that the paints flow in the desired direction.

ACTIVITY 4
ROLL-ON PAINTING WITH PRIMARY COLORS

What you need
Tempera paints—blue, yellow, and red
Mural paper (butcher paper)
Construction paper
Commercial paint rollers
Cardboard rollers

How you begin
Provide children with several sheets of mural paper; blue, yellow, and red tempera paints; and preferably commercial paint rollers (cardboard rollers can be used). Have the children work in small groups, dipping the rollers into tempera paint and pushing them around on the paper. The result is an array of various colors. A different effect is created when children drip paint on the paper and then roll it. Individual children can paint with cardboard rollers on construction paper. The paints will mix to make a variety of colors and designs.

Inferring
Encourage children to make *inferences* about the results obtained with the rollers:

> What colors do you think made purple?
> How do you think you made orange?
> Why do you think the colors is thicker on this part of the paper?
> Why do you think there is no paint on this side? Why do you think the colors didn't mingle here?

ACTIVITY 5
OBJECT PRINTING WITH PRIMARY COLORS

What you need

Tempera paint—blue, yellow, and red
Manila drawing paper
Variety of objects—hair rollers, jar tops, sponges, small
   blocks, cotton, and so forth

How you begin

Offer children red, blue, and yellow paint in small containers. Paints should be mixed to a thick consistency. Provide manila drawing paper and a variety of objects to use in printing. Tell the children to use the objects to make prints on the paper by dipping each object in the paint, placing it on the paper, then lifting it up. They can do this again and as many times as they want. Explain to the children the difference between printing and painting. Printing is putting an object down to make a print and then picking it up and putting it down again to make another print. Children will discover that they need to dip objects in paint often in order to make a recognizable print.

Observing

Encourage children to make a variety of prints. Some children will use one color, and others will use all of the colors. Talk with the children about the combination of colors and objects used to make the prints. Sometimes children have difficulty identifying the objects they use to make specific prints. Help them to examine the bottoms of objects and talk about the parts that are covered with paint. Notice that some parts may not touch the paint and therefore don't make contact with the paper. Often children place objects on top or partially on top of each other while they are printing. The result is an interesting picture that challenges children to identify the objects and colors represented.

ACTIVITY 6
STRING PAINTING WITH PRIMARY COLORS

What you need

Tempera paint—blue, yellow, and red
Manila drawing paper
String

How you begin

Give children manila drawing paper; jars of red, yellow, and blue tempera paint; and several strings. Tell the children to put a string in one of the jars until it is soaked with paint; arrange the string on the paper and then fold the paper. Pull the string through the paper. Children can vary the design by the way they arrange the string and pull it through the paper. When various colors are used, they blend to make unusual colors.

Predicting

Encourage children to make *predictions* about the resulting colors:

What colors will you use?
What colors do you think will be in your picture? Why do you think so?
How can you make orange? Purple? Green?

ACTIVITY 7
USING TEMPERA PAINT TO ADD WHITE AND BLACK TO COLORS

What you need

Easel(s)
Paint carriers for painting at tables
Tempera paints—blue, yellow, red, white, and black
Brushes—1", ¾", and ½" (long handles); ¼" and ¹/₁₆" (short handles)
Water jars
Newsprint

How you begin

Add white paint to the blue, yellow, and red paint at the easel(s) or on the table. Provide a jar of water for rinsing brushes. Observe children as they mix white paint with the other colors. Ask the children,

> What happens when you mix white with _____?
> Does white make colors lighter or darker?
> How did you make pink?
> Can you make light blue?

Comparing

Children will make wide variations in colors and begin to *compare* them: "This pink is lighter than that one." "I'm going to make very light green." "I made the lightest yellow." "Can you make this color?" One five-year-old child spent 30 minutes mixing red and white until she had the desired shade of pink. She covered the entire piece of paper with pink paint and allowed it to dry. Then she painted a red border across the bottom and with a small brush gently shook white paint on it. She said, "I mixed a pretty pink, didn't I?" The effect was lovely.

How investigation continues

Add black paint to the other colors at the easel or on the table. Encourage children to make shades of color with black as they made tints with the white paint. One five-year-old made an unusual valentine picture by encircling her green heart with grey paint surrounded by red paint. The valentine colors used by the kindergarten children in this class included orange, blue, grey, white, dark green, pink, and red.

ACTIVITY 8
USING FINGER PAINTS TO ADD WHITE AND BLACK TO COLORS

What you need
Finger paint (commercial or homemade)—blue, yellow, red, white and black
Finger paint paper

How you begin
Offer children white finger paint in addition to blue, yellow, and red finger paint.

Predicting
From their past experiences with mixing paints, children will be able to *predict* how to make light colors. Encourage experimentation with the white paint by asking,

> What happens when you use white paint?
> Can you see your finger marks in the paint?
> How can you make light blue paint? How much white paint do you need?
> Can you make light brown? How much red paint will you need? How much yellow paint? Blue paint? White paint? Did you make light brown? If you add more white paint, what will happen to the brown paint?

How investigation continues
After children have explored white paint, introduce black finger paint. Plan activities similar to those used in activity 2.

THOUGHTS ON MIXING COLORS

I have found that young children can learn to mix paints easily and effectively. Children should continue to mix paints throughout their school experiences. Unfortunately many teachers mix paints for children, denying them the opportunity to create exciting colors for themselves. A knowledge of mixing paints often leads to remarkable art work.

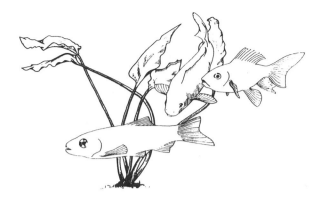

CARING FOR CLASSROOM PETS

Most teachers of young children have some kind of pet animal in the classroom. These pets range from white mice to rabbits. Too often, though, teachers have animals they don't particularly like and don't know much about. The animals may be ignored by teachers and children except at feeding time. I feel that teachers should not have animals in the classroom unless they are interested in the animals and are willing to learn all they can about them. When teachers learn about a particular animal, they sometimes become more interested in having it in the classroom. During a science workshop I stated that gerbils were exciting pets. One participant said emphatically, "Tell me what's exciting about gerbils. Just tell me!" I hope that by the end of the workshop I had convinced the teacher that gerbils were, at least, interesting.

How to choose pets

Animals that make good classroom pets are gerbils, rabbits, parakeets, guinea pigs, mice, toads, and fish. I have known several public school teachers who have successfully kept rabbits as pets. The rabbits moved freely about the classroom and used the litter provided for them. The teachers or children took the rabbits home over the weekends. Guinea pigs are friendly, do not bite, and make excellent pets, but they are messy and require a daily change of litter. Hamsters are not the best pets since they will bite and sleep in the daytime. Gerbils make very satisfactory pets. They are clean, easy to feed, affectionate, curious, sleep at night, and don't bite unless squeezed too hard or mistreated. Given water and food, they can spend the weekend at school. Goldfish are interesting, easy to take care of, colorful, and inexpensive. Although I have chosen gerbils and goldfish as examples of classroom pets, other animals can be used in the activities.

Before purchasing gerbils or goldfish from a pet store,

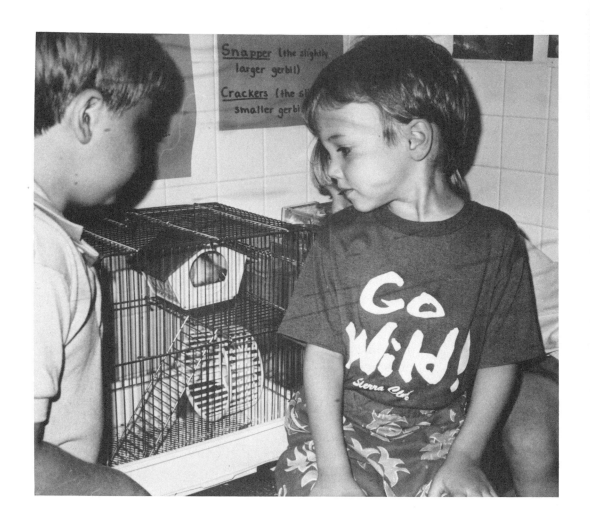

you will need to learn all you can about these animals. Pet stores sell a variety of inexpensive, informative books about pets. Other teachers who have raised gerbils and goldfish in the classroom are also good sources of information.

Science processes

Children learn through *observation* the attributes and habits of goldfish and gerbils. They *predict* what foods gerbils and goldfish will eat and what they will be doing at a specific time of day. *Space/time relations* are developed as photographs of goldfish and gerbil activities are placed in sequential order. From photographs and observations children make *inferences* about the animals such as "The gerbils like to play just like we do" and "The fish swim all the time; they must get tired." The children *talk about* the characteristics of the gerbils and fish. Understandings necessary for *classification* are developed as children discuss the ways gerbils and goldfish are alike. Seriation understandings are developed as children make *comparisons* between gerbils and goldfish. There are more differences between these animals than there are likenesses. Children experience *number* as they talk about two fish and two gerbils and as they count the number of raisins and berries dropped in the gerbils' dish. Children draw *conclusions* from their experimentations. Some conclusions children have drawn about goldfish and gerbils are "Gerbils like to play with toys" and "Goldfish move all the time."

What you need for pets activities

Two gerbils—Two males or two females will be compatible. Two are suggested since they appear to like each other's company and their interactions are interesting to watch. Gerbils may be different colors; for example, one brown and one black and white. (The activities described are not appropriate for a family of gerbils, although raising a family of gerbils is very worthwhile. Consult books on gerbils for information about raising babies.)

Gerbil cage—plastic or metal (An old aquarium with a wire top can be used.)

Water bottle

Shallow, heavy dish for food (one that the gerbils can't turn over)

Exercise wheel

Gerbil litter

Commercial gerbil food—at least two kinds

Two common or fantail goldfish

Aquarium—plastic or glass, 5–10 gal (1 gal to 1 in., or 2.5 cm, of fish)

Aquarium gravel

Several small snails

Ceramic bridge—about 4 in., or 10 cm, high

Aquatic plants—duckweed, fanwort, milfoil, or other suitable plants

Vibrator pump with air stone

Commercial fish food—at least two kinds

Fish net

51

Me and My cat

ACTIVITY 1
GETTING TO KNOW THE PETS

What you need   Two gerbils, cage, equipment, and food
Two goldfish, aquarium, equipment, and food
Felt-tip markers and/or crayons
Chart tablet (24″ × 32″), scrapbook, *or* teacher-made class
   book (tag board for cover, manila drawing paper, hole
   puncher, reinforcements for holes, large rings)

How you begin   Preparing satisfactory houses for the gerbils and goldfish
and placing them in appropriate areas of the classroom are
essential. If possible, place the gerbil cage and the aquarium in the same area of the room. You should show an interest in the animals by observing them with the children.
At first you hold the gerbils while the children pet them.
Then you should show the children how to carefully and
gently pick up and hold the gerbils. They can escape easily, and children must be supervised while holding the
pets. Children can help feed the gerbils and goldfish, clean
the gerbil cage, and change the filter in the aquarium.

Observing and communicating   Listen to the children's comments about the animals. Encourage them to *talk about* their observations by asking:

> Do both gerbils use the wheel? Why do they run on the wheel?
> How do the gerbils sleep?
> Do the gerbils play together?
> Do the goldfish play?
> Why do you think the goldfish move around the bottom of the
>   aquarium?
> Do they swim under the bridge? Rest under the bridge?
> Why do they swim to the top of the aquarium?

If children disagree about the behavior of the gerbils
and/or goldfish, ask them to *observe* the animals again.
Watch the animals with the children, and then discuss
what happened.

Communicating   Make a book of the children's observations. Let the children *dictate* what they want written in their book. Read
the book to the children, and add to it whenever the children have something to report. Children may want to *draw*
pictures for the book. One kindergarten class called their
book "The Discovery Book."

ACTIVITY 2
COMPARING GOLDFISH AND GERBILS

What you need

Two gerbils, cage, equipment, and food
Two goldfish, aquarium, equipment, and food
Polaroid camera and film
Tag board *or* posterboard for chart
Felt-tip marker

How you begin

This activity is designed to help children make comparisons between the gerbils and the goldfish. Ask the children,

> Do the gerbils and the fish behave the same way?

Discuss the differences in their behavior with the children. Tell the children you are going to take pictures with the camera of the gerbils and the goldfish at the beginning and end of the school day. As soon as the first pictures are taken, show them to the children.

Classifying and comparing

Talk about what the gerbils and the goldfish are doing:

> What are the gerbils doing?
> What are the goldfish doing?
> Are they doing the same things?

Near the end of the school day take pictures again and show them to the children. Encourage children to look for ways gerbils and goldfish are alike (basis for *classification*) and *compare* ways they are different (basis for seriation). Children have noted these similarities between gerbils and goldfish: "Both have a house." "Both eat and breathe." "Both need someone to take care of them." "Both rest sometimes." "Both have eyes and a mouth." Differences children have mentioned are as follows: "Gerbils have fur and whiskers." "Goldfish move their bodies when they rest." "Gerbils have four legs." "Goldfish have fins." "Goldfish live in water."

Comparing

Take pictures for a week. Each day place the pictures of the gerbils and the goldfish next to each other on a chart, such as that shown in the Figure. At the end of the week there will be 20 pictures, 10 of the gerbils and 10 of the goldfish. Since the pictures are in sequential order, the

DAY	Time 9AM		Time 2 PM	
Monday				
Tuesday				
Wednesday				
Thursday				
Friday				

children can make *comparisons* between the behaviors of the gerbils and the goldfish on a daily basis.

Using time relations

Encourage the use of *time relations* by asking the children questions:

> What were the gerbils doing when you came to school on Monday? Tuesday? [And so forth]
>
> What were they doing just before you went home Monday? Tuesday? [And so forth]
>
> Look at all the pictures. What were the gerbils doing most of the time?
>
> What were the goldfish doing when you came to school on Monday? Tuesday? [And so forth]
>
> What were they doing just before you went home Monday? Tuesday? [And so forth]
>
> Look at all the pictures. What were the goldfish doing most of the time?

Help the children understand that certain animal behaviors occur more often than others. One nursery school child said, "The goldfish swim, swim, swim," and a five-year-old said, "The gerbils rest most of the time."

Observing

Continue to take pictures as long as the children are interested. Encourage them to *observe* the behaviors of the gerbils and the goldfish and look for the same behaviors in the photographs.

ACTIVITY 3
FEEDING THE PETS

What you need

Two gerbils, cage, equipment, and food
Two goldfish, aquarium, equipment, and food
Books about gerbils and goldfish purchased from a pet
   store and placed on the science table or on the library
   shelf
Various kinds of vegetables and fruits (suggested by the
   children)
Chart tablet (24″ × 32″), scrapbook, *or* teacher-made class
   book (tag board for cover, manila drawing paper, hole
   puncher, reinforcements for holes, large rings)
Posterboard for chart
Felt-tip markers and/or crayons

How you begin

Children enjoy feeding the gerbils and the goldfish and
watching them eat. After the children have fed commercial food to their pets for several days, ask them,

> What do the gerbils eat?
> What do the goldfish eat?
> Where do we get their food?
> How much should we feed them?
> Where can we find information about what is good for our pets
>   to eat?

If the children don't mention books about pets, the teacher
can tell them that books have the information they need.
Pictures from books on the pets can be shown and parts of
the book read to the children. The children will learn that
goldfish need at least two kinds of commercial food and
that the water should not be polluted with other foods. It
is safe to feed gerbils parts of nonpoisonous plants.

Predicting and inferring

Talk with the children about parts of plants gerbils might
like to eat. Some suggestions children have made are lettuce, raisins, carrots, celery, blueberries, and peanuts. Encourage the children to experiment with the foods they
suggest. Each day give one of the foods to the gerbils. Ask
the children,

> How will we know that the gerbils like the food?

Some children may say that the gerbils must eat all of the
food. Tell them that most gerbils don't eat a lot of food at

one time and that if the gerbils eat part of the food, it probably means they like it. Before the children leave school remove the remaining food from the cage. Place the new food in the gerbils' dish. Encourage the children to make *predictions* about the foods by asking questions such as

Do you think the gerbils will like the _____?

The next morning examine the gerbils' dish. Encourage the childen to make *inferences* about the food by asking

How do you know the gerbil liked the _____? Didn't like the _____?

Using number

Children use *number* when they assess the amount of food in the gerbils' dish and the amount remaining the next day. In one kindergarten the children saved a few raisins from their snack. They decided to put ten raisins in a dish and leave it in the gerbils' cage until the next morning. The next day two raisins were missing from the dish. The children looked for the raisins in the gerbils' litter but didn't find any. Since the gerbils ate two raisins, the children decided they liked raisins.

Communicating

Children can *communicate* their findings verbally and/or by keeping a record of the foods the gerbils eat. The children can draw pictures of the foods for a class book. In one kindergarten the children kept a "Yes or No" chart. Each time the gerbil was offered a food, the teacher wrote the name of the food on a chart. A child put a check mark under the "Yes" column if the gerbil tasted the food. If the gerbil didn't eat any of the food, a check mark was placed under the "No" column.

How investigation continues

Continue to experiment with different foods as long as the children are interested in the activity. Later, offer the gerbils several foods they like at the same time to find out which ones they will choose.

ACTIVITY 4
WATCHING PETS PLAY

What you need

Two gerbils, cage, equipment, and food
Tin can with the tops removed (Smooth any sharp edges
    with a hammer and pliers.)
Various children's small toys
Building blocks

How you begin

Give the gerbils a tin can with the tops removed. Watch them run back and forth through the can. Sometimes they run into each other in their attempts to get through the can. Ask the children,

> Why do you think the gerbils run through the can?

Most children will say that the gerbils are playing. Talk with the children about the different ways gerbils play. Three- and four-year-old children said that gerbils "play on wheels," "run around the cage," "wrestle each other," and "dig holes in the litter."

Predicting

After discussing the children's answers ask,

> Do you think the gerbils would play with other objects?
> Which objects do you think they would like?

Most children will choose objects they use in their play. Keep a list of the objects the children mention. One kindergarten teacher's list included car, truck, ball, baby blanket, block, dish, and baby bottle. Read the list to the children, and tell them that they can take turns testing all the objects on the list. It may take several days before the gerbils explore all the objects.

Observing

Tell the children that it will be easier to see the gerbils play with the objects if they are not in their cage but in an enclosure made with building blocks. Have the children help make the enclosure, but supervise carefully to be sure it will be safe for the gerbils and that no blocks will fall on them. The block enclosure should be at least 15 inches (37.5 cm) high, but not so high that the children can't see over it. Tell them not to touch the blocks while the gerbils are in the enclosure; a block might fall on the gerbils and hurt them. Put the gerbils in the enclosure, and have the children *observe* their behavior. The gerbils will enjoy a larger home and explore the enclosure. Place the first object with the gerbils, and let the children watch what happens. Write down the children's descriptions of the gerbils' reactions to the objects so that comparisons with other objects can be made later.

Predicting and inferring

Encourage the children to make *predictions* and *inferences* about the gerbils by asking questions such as

Do you think the gerbils will play with the _____?
Why do you think so?
How do you know the gerbils like the _____?

In the kindergarten described above, the teacher placed a car in an enclosure with the gerbils. Questions asked by the teacher were "Are the gerbils curious about the car? Is one more curious than the other? How do you know they are curious? What are the gerbils doing? Do you think they are playing with the car? Why do you think so?" The children's comments were "The gerbils run over the car," "They run around the car," "Look, one is sitting on top of the car," and "They are playing 'cause they have fun on the car." The children found that the gerbils "played" with all the objects. They especially liked the baby blanket to hide under.

Comparing

Later give the gerbils a choice of three objects they liked very much. Ask the children,

Which one do they like best?
Why do you think so?

Continue experimentation with the objects throughout the year.

ACTIVITY 5
BUILDING MAZES

What you need

Two gerbils, cage, equipment, and food
Building blocks
Manila drawing paper
Felt-tip markers and/or crayons

How you begin

Ask the children how the block enclosure could be changed, and discuss their answers. Some suggestions children have given are "Make it bigger," "Use more blocks," "Build two rooms," and "Build a tunnel." Encourage the children to build other structures for the gerbils. Make certain that the enclosures are safe, and there is no danger that the blocks will fall on the gerbils.

Observing

Encourage the children to *observe* the gerbils as they interact in the enclosure by asking,

Will they move from one room to another?
Do they explore every part of the enclosure?
Do they want to get out?

Predicting

After the children have watched the gerbils in the enclosures, help the children build a simple maze for the gerbils with blocks. Explain to the children that a maze is a construction with a number of possible paths. Only one path leads to the end of the maze. Put the gerbils in the maze, and ask the children,

Do you think the gerbils will be able to go to the end of the maze?

Observing

Most gerbils have no difficulty finding their way in a simple maze. Increase the difficulty of the maze by adding to it each day. Place a little food at the end of the maze. Encourage the children to *observe* closely by asking,

Are both gerbils interested in the maze?
Do the gerbils behave as if they have been in the maze before?
Do the gerbils follow each other?

Concluding

Ask the children to draw pictures of mazes they would like to build for the gerbils. Allow several weeks to build the mazes so that all the children can have a turn. Ask questions such as

Were the gerbils able to find the food?
Why do you think the gerbils were able to find it? Weren't able to find it?

Nursery school and kindergarten children have given these explanations: "The gerbils are smart." "They like mazes." "The gerbils practiced how to work mazes." "The gerbils didn't like my maze." "The gerbils aren't hungry." "The gerbils want to play." "The gerbils don't want to work now."

How investigation continues Continue building mazes as long as the children are interested. Children's interest in mazes usually lasts throughout the year.

THOUGHTS ON CARING FOR CLASSROOM PETS

Children identify closely with animals. They should be exposed to adults who respect animals and who, in turn, can help them respect animals. In order to develop this respect and to care for the animals properly, children need to learn about the uniqueness of each kind of animal in the classroom through activities such as I have described. In addition to those, you will think of other experiments with gerbils. Experimentation with fish is more difficult for obvious reasons.

61

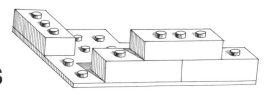

COMBINING MATERIALS

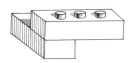

Combining materials offers children the opportunity to become more familiar with the attributes of objects. They learn that by putting materials together in various ways they can make new objects. The parts of the new objects are recognized as those that were combined to make the new objects. The form or placement may vary, but the materials remain the same.

Science processes

Noticing and describing how things are alike and how they are different are basic to developing *classification* skills. *Space/time relations* are discovered as children arrange and rearrange objects in space and *observe* the spatial transformations. They examine objects from different spatial viewpoints and notice that the relationships of the objects to each other do not change. Children *describe* the distances among materials and their locations to each other. Spatial terms are used to describe these relationships such as "on," "beside," "close to," "middle," "over," "above," and "inside." Older children may be able to anticipate how their creations will look. They may *communicate* their plans in drawings or verbally describe the order of events necessary to complete their work.

What you need for activities 1, 2, and 3

Construction toys (any with parts that may be fitted together)
Ringa-Majigs
Lincoln Logs
Crystal Climbers
Octon Builders
Pegs and peg boards
Magnetic Building Blocks
Bristle Blocks
Legos (exclude wheels)
Tinker Toys

ACTIVITY 1
EXPLORING TOY PARTS

What you need   Construction toys (any with parts that may be fitted together)

How you begin   Show the children a box containing a new construction toy.
Although the children may have seen or used the toy be-
fore, it should not be one they have used at school. Allow
them to guess what is in the box.

Predicting   If you are working with kindergarten children, tell them
to find out what is in the box by asking questions that you
can answer yes or no. Questions children typically ask are,
"Is it red? Is it wooden? Is it a block?" Three- and four-
year-olds have more difficulty than five-year-olds phrasing
questions and, therefore, should be allowed to guess
freely. Focus children's attention on the contents of the
box by asking,

> What kind of toy would fit in this box?
> Would it be a large toy? A small toy?
> Could the toy be bigger than this box? Smaller?

If there is a picture or symbol on the box, the children can
use it as a clue to the box's content. Give additional clues,
if necessary, until the children guess the contents of the
box.

Communicating   Discuss the new toy:

> What is it called?
> How is it used?
> How do the pieces fit together?
> Can more than one thing be made with the pieces?

After discussion of the new toy, ask,

> Are there any toys in the room like this one?
> Do they have parts?
> Can you fit them together?

Tell the children the new toy will be placed in the manip-
ulations center for them to play with later. Allow each
child to choose a toy, bring it to the group, and show and
tell how it can be taken apart and put together.

Classifying

Most children will choose some kind of construction toy or puzzle. A few children may bring a toy with a "belong to" relationship, such as a doll and doll clothes, rather than a "fit together relationship" such as Legos or Bristle Blocks. Accept whatever the children bring since toys may have a "belong to" as well as a "fit together" relationship. The purpose is to look for objects that are *like* the new construction toy. These objects have more than one part and can be put together (combined) and taken apart.

Observing and using spatial relations

Encourage the children to play with and talk about the different toys. Ask questions to help them *observe* the various *spatial relationships*:

How did you fit these pieces together?
Would they fit if you put them on top of each other? Beside each other?
Are the pieces the same size?
Do all the pieces fit together?

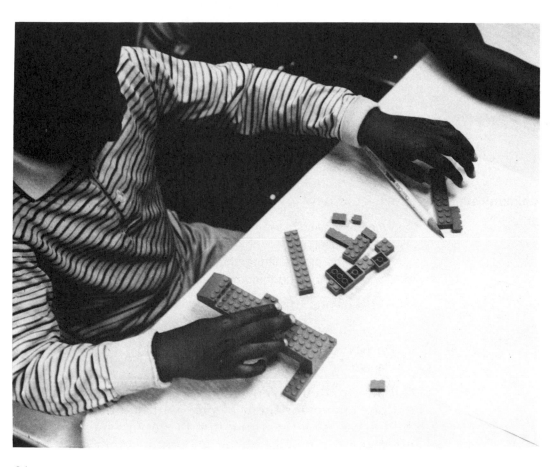

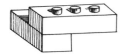

ACTIVITY 2
DESCRIBING TOY STRUCTURES

What you need

Construction toys (any with parts that may be fitted together)

How you begin

Encourage the children to build with their favorite construction toys. Ask questions such as

What are these toys called?
Why are they called construction toys?
How do the parts fit together?
Can you combine them in some way?
Can you see the parts after you have combined them?

Classifying and comparing

Children will notice and describe how the parts look *alike* and *different* in their constructions. One four-year-old child said, "I can't see the red block. It's covered up." A classmate responded, "It's still there, but you can't see it." The teacher asked, "Will it look the same when you take it apart?" The child took his construction apart, looked at the block in question, and said, "Sure."

Children probably will use the construction toys to make houses, boats, rockets, spaceships, planes, airports, and garages. Usually dramatic play follows with the children's favorite creations. You should not interrupt or discourage dramatic play with construction toys but take advantage of the opportunities to help children notice and describe how the toys are alike and different.

How are the _____ and the _____ alike? Different?
Was the _____ made with large or small blocks?
Would it look different if it were made with the small [or large] blocks?"

One five-year-old child *compared* his spaceship with another child's spaceship. He said, "I used lots of big pieces and she used little ones, but they're the same size."

65

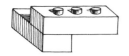

ACTIVITY 3
USING CONSTRUCTION TOYS IN NEW WAYS

What you need

Construction toys (any with parts that may be fitted together)
Manila drawing paper
Felt-tip markers and/or crayons

How you begin

Encourage the children to use construction toys in new ways. The purpose of the above activity is to help children learn more about the attributes of objects, notice likenesses and differences between and among objects, and observe objects from different spatial viewpoints. The kind of toys used by the children will to some extent determine your guidance techniques. If you say, "Find the short, yellow Legos" this statement applies only to Legos; however, if you say, "How are these pieces the same? Find all the pieces like this one," the statement may refer to any number of construction toys. The following are examples of activities that can be used with most construction toys. You can adapt the procedures to use with your classroom materials.

Classifying

Place a construction toy on a table or on the floor and ask the children to find two pieces that are alike in some way. Encourage the development of *classification* skills by asking children to describe how the parts are alike:

Are they the same color? Size? Shape? Material?
Put all the parts that are alike in some way together.

Allow the children to explain why they grouped the objects as they did. Accept the children's reasons for grouping the objects. Then ask,

Can you put the objects that are alike in some way into other groups?

Most five-year-olds and a few four-year-olds will be able to place an object in more than one group of like objects. After children have placed like objects together, tell them to combine the parts that are alike to make anything they want to make.

Although most young children classify by color, the

construction pieces may or may not be the same color and size. Children may place small and large pieces of the same color together, small or large pieces of different colors together, or small or large pieces of the same color together.

Using spatial relations

Encourage children to look at their constructions from different *spatial* viewpoints by asking,

> Did the parts of your toy change when you combined them?
> Put your toy on the tile area. Is it the same toy?
> Put it on the rug. Is it the same toy?
> Turn your toy sideways. Is it the same toy?
> Take a part off. Is it the same toy?
> Put the part back at the same place. Is it the same toy?
> Put the part at a different place. Is it the same toy?

Many five-year-old children will insist that the object changes when its position changes. Some children will say that the object remains the same. In one kindergarten classroom, the teacher encouraged the children to walk around their toys and look carefully at them from different spatial positions. After one child walked around her toy and looked at it carefully, she said, "It's the same toy that I made at the table this morning."

Nursery school children will give various answers to spatial questions based upon their unique thinking at their stage of development. One three-year-old, when asked if her toy changed when turned around, said, "It's my house," and another child said, "It doesn't want to be another toy." Both answers were based upon egocentric thought and the latter also on a belief in animism. One four-year-old child said that his toy, placed in a sunny area of the room, had changed because, "It's all shiny."

Communicating

In one kindergarten the teacher asked a group of children to *draw* pictures to show what they planned to make with Legos. A few pictures were detailed, but most showed an outline of a front view of the proposed construction. The children's final products were amazingly like their drawings. One child added parts to her construction that were not on her drawing. As she added each part to her construction, she returned to her drawing and added the new part. Young children, I have found, are able to *describe* and represent future events verbally and on paper, with, for the most part, unusual accuracy.

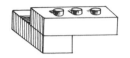

ACTIVITY 4
BUILDING BOX STRUCTURES

What you need
Small cardboard, plastic, Styrofoam, and wooden boxes—
variety of sizes and shapes
Glue
Manila drawing paper
Felt-tip markers and/or crayons

How you begin
Give children an assortment of small boxes, preferably without labels. Do not use any medicine boxes. If boxes without labels are unavailable, you may use boxes from toothpaste, shoes, cosmetics, and pencils.

Classifying and comparing
Encourage the children to talk about how the boxes are *alike* and *different* by asking such questions as

What do you think is inside the box?
What material is the box made of?
Are all of the boxes made of cardboard? [A few should be plastic, Styrofoam, or wooden.]
Can you see through any of the boxes?
Are the boxes the same size? Shape?
Put the boxes that are alike in some way together. Why didn't you include these boxes? How are they different?

Using spatial relations
Then ask the children to combine the boxes to make any kind of construction they want. Comment on the various constructions as the children combine the boxes:

You made a tall structure. How did you make it?
Your building is long and flat. How did you combine the boxes?
What would happen if you moved this box here?
Did you stack them? Put them in a row? Close or far apart?
Can you combine the same boxes to make something else?
Would you like to draw a picture of how you want it to look?
What is the large box close to? Beside? Above? Under?
Do you want to move it?

Children will notice that moving one or more boxes changes the appearance of the structures and the relation of the boxes to each other. When the children are satisfied with their combinations of boxes, have them glue the boxes together to make permanent structures. Let the children combine boxes as long as they are interested. Introduce a few different boxes each day.

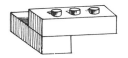

ACTIVITY 5
PASTING COLORED PAPER STRIPS

What you need

Construction paper strips (1″ × 10″, or 2.54 cm × 25.4 cm)—
   various colors
Manila drawing paper
Paste

How you begin

Give children different colored strips of construction paper and a piece of manila drawing paper. Tell the children to combine as many paper strips as they want and in
any way that they want. After the children decide what
they want, tell them to paste the strips onto the drawing
paper. The children's ability to handle paste and paper and
use these materials creatively will depend upon their eye-
hand coordination and their experience.

**Using spatial
relations**

Observe the children as they work. Do any children fold
or twist the strips of paper? Paste them flat on the paper?
Paste them on top of each other? Paste them together to
make longer strips? Extend the strips beyond the edges of
the paper? You should comment on the unique ways the
children use paper strips. One nursery school teacher
made the following comments as he observed a group of
three- and four-year-olds: "Jean is putting some of the
strips on top of each other. Peter's strip goes up into the
air. Alice is combining paper strips by twisting them
around each other. Jim is gluing his strips together." Allow children to experiment with paper strips as long as
they are interested.

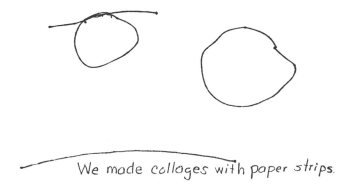

We made collages with paper strips.

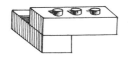

ACTIVITY 6
MAKING A TALL PICTURE

What you need

Construction paper strips (1″ × 10″, or 2.54 cm × 25.4 cm)—one color
Construction paper sheets—different colors from strips
Paste

How you begin

After children have become familiar with pasting paper strips on paper, give them strips of the same color and a piece of construction paper of a different color. Tell the children to combine the paper strips to make a picture that goes up high into the air.

Using spatial relations

Observe the children to find out how they initially solve the problem. Sometimes children paste one end of a paper strip on construction paper and, with puzzled looks, hold the loose end above the paper. Some children make a loop and paste both ends on the paper so that the strip is several inches high. A few children paste the strips flat on the paper. Teachers can encourage "tall" constructions by asking,

> What happens when you fold a paper strip?
> Can you fold it on both ends? In the middle? Back and forth?
> Can you make the strips stand up on the paper?
> Can you think of other ways to make your strips stand up?

One three-year-old pasted strip after strip on top of each other until she had a stack. She was pleased with the results and said, "I made a wall."

Observing and using spatial relations

Ask children questions to help them *observe* the *spatial transformations* that occur as they combine the strips,

> How did the strips look before you pasted them on the paper?
> How do they look now?
> What did you do to change them?

Accept the children's explanations for the ways (twist, fold, bend, pull, fasten) they changed the paper strips. One four-year-old explained, "I pulled it this way. I folded it and pasted it down." A five-year-old said, "I pasted lots of strips together. Then I pasted one end down and made a loop. Then I pasted that end down." Help children notice

70

the positions of the paper strips in relation to each other by asking questions such as

> Do any of the paper strips touch each other?
> Are the paper loops beside each other? Above each other? Under each other? On top of each other?

Children's pictures can be observed from above, at an angle, upside down, and from the side. Some children will say that their pictures are no longer the same when viewed from different angles. Children's pictures should be displayed as they were made with the base on a flat surface.

How investigation continues To vary the activity using the same material, ask the children to make a short picture that "goes across the paper." When the questions are modified, the same teaching techniques used for making a "tall" picture are appropriate.

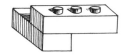

ACTIVITY 7
WORKING WITH WHOLES AND PIECES

What you need   Construction paper (9″ × 12″, or 22.86 cm × 30.5 cm)—
various colors
Paste
Crepe, tissue, and glossy paper
Newspaper
Colored foil

How you begin   Tell the children to choose two pieces of colored construction paper. Ask the children:

Are the papers the same size?
How do you know?

Encourage them to put the pieces of paper on top of each other and notice that the papers are the same size. Have them choose one of the pieces of paper and cut or tear it. When they are finished, tell them to put all of the pieces on the big sheet of paper.

Using space/time relations   Let the children divide the paper into as many parts as they wish. Encourage them to fit all the pieces on the large piece of construction paper. Three-year-olds may solve the problem by pasting the pieces on top of each other. This is a logical solution for them at their stage of development. One four-year-old decided before he tore his paper that he would make a puzzle to fit the whole sheet of paper. He carefully tore his paper into three parts and pasted them on the paper with a small space between each. He said, "I made a puzzle with my paper." In one nursery school all the children succeeded in fitting their pieces on the whole sheets of construction paper. Some children tore their paper into strips and made loops to glue on the sheet. Other children carefully fitted each piece on the paper, while a few children glued pieces on top of each other to make them fit.

Communicating   Encourage children to *tell* how they arranged their pieces of paper. Ask questions such as

How did you fit this piece next to that one? What did you do?
Did you have to move the pieces around on the paper until they
    fit?
Can you see all of the pieces you used? Why? Why not?

Observing

Children can *look at* their pictures from different *spatial* viewpoints. Guidance techniques similar to those in activity 6 may be used.

How investigation continues

As long as they are interested, allow children to work with cut or torn pieces of construction paper and a whole piece of construction paper. Vary the activities by using other materials such as the papers and foil listed above.

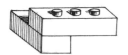

ACTIVITY 8
MAKING COLLAGES

What you need

Styrofoam trays
Five boxes
Manila drawing paper
Glue
Variety of collage materials such as buttons, sparkling sequins, Styrofoam multishaped pieces, small pieces of construction paper, feathers, colored macaroni, cotton balls, assorted stickers, small pieces of colorful fabric

How you begin

Provide the children with an assortment of collage materials. Place one kind of collage material in each of five boxes. Give children Styrofoam trays, and ask them to choose from the various boxes those materials that they think they will need.

Observing

Talk with the children as they make their collages on paper or in the trays. You could say, for example,

You used red beads. Did you use red anywhere else in your picture?
What colors are you planning to use in your picture?
What shape is this button?
Are there any other materials that are round?
Which materials do you plan to place beside each other? Why?
This feather is fluffy. Do you see any other fluffy, soft materials?

Communicating

Encourage the children to *talk about* the materials and their positions in relation to each other. One teacher taped children as they described their pictures. The tape was played when the children's parents viewed the pictures during an open house.

THOUGHTS ON COMBINING MATERIALS

There are many activities that help children become keen observers, learn the attributes of objects, and become aware of space/time relations. Children also have the opportunity to express themselves creatively as they apply their unique ideas to their constructions. I have found the above activities to be some of the most successful.

EXPERIMENTING
WITH BALANCE

Children as young as <u>three years</u> enjoy teacher-made or commercial equal-arm balances. They like to place objects on either side of a balance and watch what happens to the arm. They are fascinated when one end touches the floor. They try to "make the arm straight" or balance it by changing objects on either side of the balance. The word "balance" is seldom used by them, but through experimentation they begin to understand the concept of balancing.

You may initiate several activities to broaden young children's understanding of balance. Crude but efficient balances can be made with unit blocks. A long block can serve as a beam and a short one as a fulcrum. Objects may be placed on either side to make the beam balance. Removal of one or more objects will upset the balance. Commercial balances should also be provided to give children a variety of balancing experiences. Outdoor balancing activities involve children's whole bodies as they attempt to balance a low beam on the ground.

Science processes

Careful *observation* is necessary for children to ascertain the results of their experimentations. *Prediction* is used as objects are placed on and removed from balances. When children determine the desired distances of objects from the fulcrum, they are using *space/time relations* and a form of *measurement*. Objects and actions are *classified* as effective or ineffective according to their usefulness in balancing. Children are encouraged to make *inferences* when you ask,

> How can you balance the beam when one end is shorter than the other?
> What can you put on this end to balance the beam?

Five-year-olds and older fours may want to draw pictures to *communicate* what they are doing with the balances.

They may dictate what is happening in their pictures for you to write down. Some children may want to dictate their findings about balancing to be included in a class book.

What you need for balancing activities

Materials used in balancing activities may consist entirely of blocks, classroom objects, and teacher-made equipment. If possible, also provide a commercial equal-arm balance.

ACTIVITY 1
BALANCING BLOCKS

What you need   Unit blocks—several pairs of one short block (1⅜″ high) and one long block

How you begin   Put a short unit block (fulcrum) under a long unit block (beam). Place one end of the long block on the floor. Ask the children,

Can you move the long block so that both ends are off the floor?

Observing   Encourage experimentation by asking questions such as

What will happen if you move the long block?
What will happen if you move the long block to one end of the small block?

Five-year-old and four-year-old children may already know how to balance the block or will find out soon after they begin exploring. Three-year-old children may balance the block through trial and error. If the children do not use the term "balance," you can introduce it by referring to the block as balanced or not. Some children may discover that another way to balance the long block is to move the shorter block. Set up several arrangements of long and short unit blocks. Allow the children to explore the various arrangements until they have balanced the long block.

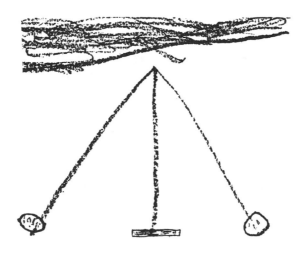

ACTIVITY 2
USING OBJECTS TO BALANCE

What you need
Unit blocks—several pairs of one short block (1⅜″ high) and one long block
Smaller unit blocks
Cube blocks
Wooden dominoes

How you begin
Use the unit blocks and set up several balances. Introduce cube blocks, wooden dominoes, or small unit blocks. Encourage children to experiment with the materials by asking,

What will happen if you put a domino on one end of the block?
Can you use the little blocks to balance the long block?

One four-year-old placed a block on one end of the long block and immediately placed one on the other end to balance it. Another four-year-old put several blocks on one end of the beam. The teacher asked, "Can you make the block even? Will it balance?" The child said, "Yes," and placed the same number of blocks on the other end. Pointing to each block she explained, "I put these blocks here and the same blocks on this end so it would balance."

Observing and predicting
Encourage *observation* and *prediction* by asking the children,

How can you balance the block?
How do you know it is balanced?
What happens when you put the same number of blocks on each end?
What happens when you have more blocks on one end than on the other end?

One five-year-old noticed that the block was not balanced even though there were identical blocks on both sides. (One set of blocks was closer to the fulcrum). She took the fulcrum (short block) and moved it until the beam was balanced.

ACTIVITY 3
TRYING DIFFERENT ARRANGEMENTS

What you need

Unit blocks—variety of short and long blocks
Commercial equal-arm balances
Classroom objects—variety for balancing
Chart tablet (24″ × 32″), scrapbook, *or* teacher-made class book (tag board for cover, manila drawing paper, hole puncher, reinforcements for holes, large rings)
Felt-tip markers and/or crayons

How you begin

Continue the balancing activities by providing children with a variety of unit blocks. They will make their own balances with long and short blocks. If you have not introduced the terms "beam" and "fulcrum," use them now as you ask questions about the balancing activities. Experimentation can begin with questions such as

Can you balance the beam?
Can you make one side of the beam go down?
What will happen if you move the fulcrum?

Observing and predicting

Encourage *observation* and *prediction* by supplying children with new objects to use in balancing. Ask questions such as

Will the same kind of objects on each end balance the beam?
Will different kinds of objects on both ends balance the beam?

How you continue

Give the children commercial equal-arm balances to use with the materials. Ask questions to encourage observation:

Can you balance the beam?
What kind of objects did you use?
Which side is heavier?
Why do you think so?

Inferring

Encourage children to make *inferences* by asking questions such as

Why do you think the beam is balanced?
What would happen if you took the objects away from one end?
Do these balances work the same way as the balances made with blocks?

80

Classifying

Encourage children to choose objects in the room to use in their experimentation. Discuss the objects and arrangements:

Which ones were successful?
Which ones were unsuccessful? Why?

Placing objects and arrangements in successful and unsuccessful categories is a form of *classification*.

Inferring

Allow children to continue to experiment with all the available balances. Question the children as they work with the balances to determine if they are aware that it takes more weight on the short end of a beam to make it balance and that if objects are added to one end of the beam, they must be added to the other end to maintain balance.

Communicating

Encourage children to *communicate* their findings to each other. Several five-year-old children drew pictures of their arrangements, and the teacher put the pictures in a class book. If there are differences of opinion, urge the children to talk about them and to demonstrate what they have learned from their experimentations. One kindergarten teacher learned that there was general agreement among the children on the requirements for saying a board was balanced, "The ends are off the ground."

How investigation continues

If possible, allow the children to take some of the balances outside and experiment with objects found on the playground or brought from the classroom.

ACTIVITY 4
ANTICIPATING OUTCOMES

What you need   Balance beam (3″ wide) and fulcrum; long block (5½″ × ¾″
                    × 44″) from a hollow block set with a unit block (1⅜″
                    high) as a fulcrum; and/or wooden board with cleats (76″
                    × 15″ × 14″, usually available with portable metal base)
                    with a unit block (1⅜″ high) as a fulcrum
                    Classroom objects—variety for balancing
                    Manila drawing paper
                    Felt-tip markers and/or crayons
                    Wooden dominoes

How you begin   In the classroom place a balance beam with its fulcrum
                    and/or a long board with a unit block as a fulcrum.

Predicting   Encourage the children to place the fulcrum in different
                    positions in order to balance or unbalance the board. When
                    the board is unbalanced, ask,

>   How could we balance the board?
>   What objects can we use?
>   Will we need the same objects on both ends?

Encourage the children to suggest kinds of objects, how
many, and where they should be placed on the board. By
now children have learned which objects are heavy, medium, and light.

Communicating Encourage <u>five-year-old</u> children to *draw* an arrangement
                   of objects that they think will balance the board. Ask them
                   to *describe* their arrangements and explain why they think
                   their placement of objects will be successful. Allow the
                   children to discuss the arrangements and, if necessary,
                   make suggestions for adding, moving, or removing ob-
                   jects. In one kindergarten three children agreed on an ar-
                   rangement and shared their drawing with the other
                   children.

Predicting   After the children have discussed various arrangements, try
                   out each prediction with objects. Some <u>five-year-olds</u> won't
                   want to make drawings but will make verbal *predictions*.
                   <u>Three-</u> and <u>four-year-old</u> children will make verbal pre-

82

dictions and enjoy trying them out. One group of kindergarten children placed wooden dominoes on each side of the board until it balanced. Later they balanced the board by standing dominoes side to side across it.

Communicating This activity gives children the opportunity to work together, share ideas, *discuss* different viewpoints, and try out ideas. It also gives children an opportunity to reflect on their experimentations and use what they have learned in new situations.

ACTIVITY 5
USING THEIR BODIES TO BALANCE

What you need

Balance beam (3″ wide) and fulcrum; long block (5½″ × ¾″ × 44″) from a hollow block set with a unit block (1⅜″ high) as a fulcrum; and/or wooden board with cleats (76″ × 15″ × 14″, usually available with portable metal base) with a unit block (1⅜″ high) as fulcrum
Manila drawing paper
Felt-tip markers and/or crayons

How you begin

In the playground place a long board or a balance beam on a fulcrum with one end of the board or beam touching the ground. The fulcrum should be no more than two or three inches high. Ask the children,

Can you keep both ends of the board from touching the ground?

One four-year-old moved a balance beam board and lay flat on it. She said, "Hey! I'm balancing." Another child moved the balance beam until it balanced. Then he walked down one side of the beam until it touched the ground. The teacher asked, "Why did the board go down?" He replied, "I walked on it. There's no one on the other end."

Observing and using spatial relations

Encourage the children to *observe* each other as they attempt to balance on the board. Ask questions that invite children to consider various *spatial* arrangements:

Why do you think _____ and _____ balance the board?
Why do you think the board falls when _____ and _____ are on it?
What happened when _____ moved to the end of the board?
Can you balance the board by putting one foot on either end?
Will the board balance if one foot is near the end and the other foot is near the middle of the board?

Predicting

Children should be encouraged to make *predictions*. You can ask,

What do you think will happen if the board is moved?
What will happen if you stand near the middle?
How many children do you think it will take to balance the board?

As children explore different board arrangements, their predictions will become more accurate.

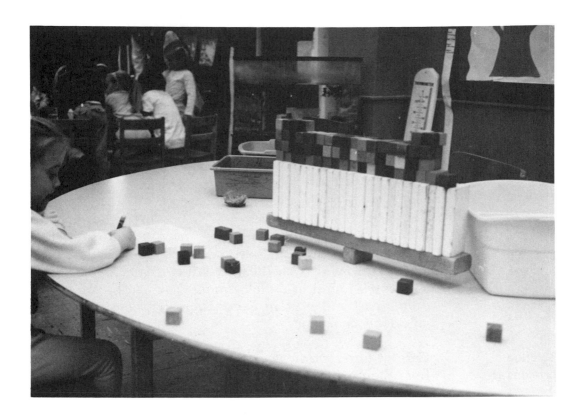

Inferring

Help children to make *inferences* about their observations by asking questions such as

Why do you think the board is balanced?
Why do you think _____ and _____ can't balance the board?
    What can they do to balance it?
Why do you think so?

Communicating

Children will make predictions and inferences almost simultaneously and *communicate* their findings verbally to each other and the teacher. Older children may want to draw their arrangements.

THOUGHTS ON EXPERIMENTING WITH BALANCE

Balancing activities may continue for several weeks depending on the interests and ages of the children. Interest may be renewed as children attempt to balance a seesaw. They soon learn that each end of the seesaw must have approximately the same weight.

INVESTIGATING SAND

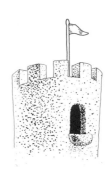

Before their first school experience, most children have become familiar with sand. They have felt the sensation of sand between their toes and made sand castles, pies, and cakes. Sand is an inexpensive and versatile medium commonly found in the classroom. You can broaden children's past and present experiences by focusing on specific aspects of sand.

Science processes

Careful *observation* is necessary if children are to learn from their experiences with sand. They develop the basis for *classification* by exploring the attributes of sand. They observe, feel, and smell sand. They listen to sand particles falling from high above or close to the sand table. They learn what happens when wet and dry sand are placed in sieves, funnels, and colanders. Understandings necessary for seriation are developed as children make *comparisons* between dry sand and wet sand, big and small holes, and large and small containers. They *predict* how sand will sound when it falls from sieves, colanders, and funnels. Children use *measurement* and *number* when they choose the container that holds the most and least sand and count the number of cups it takes to fill a container. They develop *spatial relations* as they drop sand from far away and close to the sand table. Children make *inferences* to explain why sand flows freely from some containers and not from others. Children *talk about* their experiences with teachers and peers. They demonstrate the success of their handmade sieves.

What you need for sand activities

Sand table, combination sand/water table, large cardboard boxes, *or* large, transparent plastic containers
Sand suitable for a sandbox—can be purchased from a building supplies company

ACTIVITY 1
DESCRIBING SAND

What you need

Sand table, large cardboard boxes, *or* large plastic
containers
Sand

How you begin

Fill the sand table or large plastic container with sand.
Children like sand and will gravitate to the sand table.
Observe the children as they move their hands in the sand,
cup sand in their hands, and drop it in mid air over the
sand table. Listen to the chidren's comments about sand;
some examples: "The sand feels good." "I like to watch
the sand fall. It works like rain." "I squeeze my fingers together so the sand won't come out."

**Observing and
communicating**

Say to the children,

Bury your hands in the sand. How does the sand feel?

Children may *describe* sand as "cool," "heavy," "funny,"
"good," "sandy," and "dark." Then say to the children,

Rub sand between your hands. How does it feel?

Children have said sand feels "gritty," "funny," "sharp,"
"rough," and "hard." Ask the children,

What color is the sand?

Most children will describe sand as "brown," "whitish,"
"brownish," or "beige." One child said, "I saw white sand
at the beach," and another child, who was born in Hawaii,
said, "I've seen black sand."

Inferring

Tell the children that it isn't safe to taste sand since it isn't
edible. Ask them,

How do you think the sand will taste? Will smell?

They may be able to *infer* from smelling sand how it tastes.
Children have described sand as smelling like "dirt,"
"sand," "earth," "bad," and "good." They decided sand
tasted like dirt since that's how it smelled.

ACTIVITY 2
EXPLORING FURTHER

What you need

Sand table, large cardboard boxes, *or* large plastic containers
Sand
Paper towels
Magnifying glasses

How you begin

While children are at the sand table, encourage them to move their hands in the sand.

Classifying

Help them explore the *properties* of sand by asking,

What happens to the sand when you lift your hands straight up?
What happens to the sand when you bend your hands? Move your hands back and forth in the sand?
Move your fingers in the sand. How does the sand look?

One five-year-old child said, "If you hold your hands straight up the sand won't fall off," and another child said, "If you open your fingers it will." After moving her hands back and forth in the sand, one four-year-old child said, "The sand gets under my fingernails." The teacher asked, "Why do you think it does?" The child replied, "Because I push the sand with my hands." Children will notice that moving their hands in the sand produces a smooth area. Other comments include: "Fingers make roads in sand." "You can make your handprint in sand if it's not too dry." "Moving your hands over sand makes it smooth." "If you hold sand in your hand and drop it, you'll hear a soft sound."

Observing

Encourage the children to *observe* the sand closely. Tell each child to spread a little sand on a paper towel and look at it with a magnifying glass. Say to the children,

What do you see when you look at it with the magnifying glass?

The children will observe that sand is composed of many small parts. One five-year-old child said, "Look at the little rocks," and another child said, "There are little bits of things." Tell the children that little rocks make sand. Then have them put the sand in a pile, and ask,

Can you see the rocks now?

One child said, "No;" another, "I can if I look real close."

ACTIVITY 3
WIPING SAND OFF

What you need   Sand table, large cardboard boxes, *or* large plastic con-
tainer
Sand
Paper towels
Aluminum foil
Construction paper
Wax paper

How you begin   After the children have had their hands in the sand, give
each child a paper towel and tell them to wipe the sand off
their hands. Are your hands clean?

The children will notice that most of the sand is on the
paper towel or on the floor. There is still some sand on
their hands. One child said, "When I'm outside in the
sandpile, I wipe my hands on the grass," and another child
said, "I'm going to wash my hands."

Predicting   Encourage children to use other materials to wipe their
hands and to *predict* which ones will get the sand off.
They will find that aluminum foil, construction paper, and
wax paper will remove most of the sand. Three- and four-
year-old children were surprised to find that sand fell off
the materials they rubbed their hands on. They expected
the sand to stay on the materials as water would. To help
the children make inferences, you can ask,

Why is there sand on the floor?
Why doesn't it stick to the paper?

Children have offered these explanations: "Paper brushes
sand off." "Sand is little pieces." "Sand can't stick to paper."

ACTIVITY 4
ANTICIPATING OUTCOMES

What you need

Sand table, large cardboard boxes, *or* large plastic containers
Sand
Plastic cups
Large and small plastic containers, preferably
    transparent—jars, bottles, bowls, food keepers
Milk cartons—quart, pint, half-pint
Commercial equal-arm balance

How you begin

Provide children with plastic cups, large and small plastic containers, and milk cartons to use in the sand. Observe and listen to the children as they play with the sand and containers. Some comments children have made are the following: "Watch me pour sand in the cup." "I put five cups of sand in the bowl." "My jar is bigger than yours." "This is too much sand for the bowl. It's too small." "My carton is heavy."

Using number and measuring

Ask questions to help children develop *number* relations and use *measurement:*

> Which carton holds the most sand? The least? How do you know?
> How many cups of sand do you think it will take to fill this container?
> Which container do you think holds more sand?

Children discover by experimentation that larger containers hold more sand than smaller containers. They learn that it is difficult to know which of two similar containers holds more sand. They are often fooled by perception just as adults sometimes misjudge the amount a container will hold. One five-year-old child said, "My container holds more sand than Jane's." The teacher asked, "How do you know?" He said, "She poured her sand in my container and it didn't fill it. So mine holds more."

Predicting and comparing

Encourage children to *compare* the weights of various containers of sand. Ask the children,

> Are the containers heavier when they are empty or filled with sand?

Children know through experience that an empty container is lighter than a filled one. Encourage children to *predict* which container of sand is heavier. Ask the children,

Which container of sand is heavier? This one or that one?

Children can compare masses by holding a container in each hand. It is sometimes difficult to know which one is heavier when the containers are close to the same weight. One four-year-old suggested, "Let's put them on the equal-arm balance." The children were surprised to find that their predictions were not always correct. Sand may be poured directly into the balance pans. Children enjoy adding to and removing sand from the pans until they balance.

How investigation continues

Allow children to compare sand masses as long as they are interested. Suggest they first predict which container is the heavier by holding one in each hand.

ACTIVITY 5

EXPERIMENTING WITH COLANDERS, SIEVES, AND FUNNELS

What you need

Sand table, large cardboard boxes, *or* large plastic
    containers
Sand
Colanders
Sieves
Funnels

How you begin

Add colanders, sieves, and funnels to the sand table. Observe and listen to children as they play with the equipment. Children will discover that, unlike water, sand won't come out of the sieves and colanders without shaking them.

Inferring and comparing

Encourage children to experiment with the equipment and to make *inferences* and *comparisons* (basis for seriation) by asking,

> How does the sand look coming through the colander? The sieve? The funnel?
> Does all of the sand go out of the funnel? Why do you think so?
> Does all the sand go through the colander? The sieve?
> Why do you think there is more sand left in the sieve than in the colander?

Typically children explain like this: "The holes in the colanders are big. The sieve has little holes." "There are rocks in the sieve, you can see them." "The rocks are too big to go through the sieve." "The sand coming out of the sieve is thinner. 'Cause the holes are littler than the holes in the colander." "Lots of sand comes out of the funnel. It has a big hole."

Using spatial relations

Tell the children to shake the colanders and sieves gently since the sand inside also makes a sound. Ask the children,

> What kind of sound do you hear when the sand falls on the sand in the sand table?

Children will discover that softer sounds are made when sand falls from the sieves than from the colanders or funnels. Encourage the development of *spatial relations* by asking the children to listen to the sounds of the sand falling near and far away from the sand table. Children have commented: "The sand sounds like rain." "You can't hear it close to the sand. It's so soft." "The sand in the sieve is real quiet. If you let it fall from far away it sounds louder when it hits the sand table."

ACTIVITY 6
EXPERIMENTING WITH THE FLOW OF SAND

What you need Sand table, large cardboard boxes, *or* large plastic
containers
Sand
Styrofoam trays
Milk cartons—quart, pint, half-pint
Small plastic bags
Plastic lids
Pencils
Hammers
Nails—variety of sizes
Construction paper
Tape or stapler

How you begin Give children Styrofoam trays, milk cartons, small plastic
bags, and plastic lids. Provide children with pencils, hammers, and a variety of nails. Allow them to punch or nail
holes in the materials. Supervise the children who are using nails and hammers.

Comparing Encourage the children to *compare* the holes by asking,

What size holes did you make? Big? Little? Medium?
Did you use a pencil or a nail?
Which nail did you use?

Inferring Have the children experiment by putting sand in the various items. Ask questions to help them make *inferences:*

Why do you think the sand goes through these containers?
Why do you think the sand won't go through those containers?
How could you make the sand come out? How could you make
it come out faster? Slower?
How could you make the holes bigger?

Allow interested children to make larger holes or holes in
additional containers.

**Using spatial
relations** Encourage the development of spatial relations by saying,

Hold the _____ close to the sand. How does the sand sound
when it falls on the sand in the sand table?

Hold the _____ far away from the sand. How does the sand
   sound when it falls on the sand in the sand table?

Children like to catch sand in their hands as their classmates shake the various containers. One three-year-old put
his hands under the sand and said, "How does the sand
sound on me?"

Comparing

Provide construction paper, and ask children to make a
cone by rolling the paper and taping or stapling the seam.
Talk about the sand as it falls through the paper funnel:

   Is there a large stream of sand? Small?
   Is the hole big? Little?

ACTIVITY 7
USING WET SAND

What you need

Sand table, large cardboard boxes, *or* large plastic
    containers
Sand
Water in sprinkling cans *or* small containers
Sieves
Funnels
Milk cartons—half-pint
Small containers—pans, cups, pots, cans
Sand molds—letters, shapes
Small classroom objects, such as wooden block, unifix
    block, felt-tip-marker top, cookie cutter, crayon, hair
    roller, plastic fruits, cooking and eating utensils, doll-
    house furniture

How you begin

Ask the children to wet the sand with sprinkling cans or
small containers of water until the sand will stay together
when they press it between their hands.

**Observing and
using spatial
relations**

Help the children to *observe* the charcteristics of wet sand.
Tell them to press their hands in the wet sand and look at
the results. One three-year-old said, "My hand's in the
sand," and a four-year-old said, "That's my print. I'm going
to make more hands." Tell the children to make their
handprints again. Have them walk around the table several times, stop, and find their handprint. Ask the children,

    How do you know it's your handprint?

One child said, "It looks like it." Another child said, "My
hand fits in this print." Most children will put their hand
in the print to make sure it's the right size.
    Then ask the children to find an object in the room to
press in the sand, and talk about the imprints:

    Which one was made by a _____? How do you know?
    Look at all of the imprints. Are some imprints easier to recog-
        nize than others?
    Why do you think so?

Children will discover imprints made by smooth objects
are easier to identify. It often is more difficult to ascertain

the imprint of an uneven object since only a part of the object may be imprinted in the sand.

Inferring

Give the children sieves and funnels to use in the wet sand. Encourage them to expand their explorations and make *inferences:*

> You put the sand in the sieve. Why do you think the sand didn't come through?
>
> Try the funnel. Will the sand fall through it? Why do you think so?

Children have answered: "The sand is pasted together." "Wet sand sticks together." "If you want to use the sieve, you'll have to let the sand dry."

Communicating

Children need little encouragement to play with wet sand. Provide them with milk cartons and other containers, and tell them to press the sand into a milk carton; then to turn it over and take the carton off.

> What shape do you see?
>
> How many different shapes can you make with the containers?
>
> What can you make with your hands?

Children *talk about* what they are going to make with the wet sand: "I need a big bowl to make a big cake." "I like this sand. I can make a castle."

How experimentation continues

Allow children to experiment with wet sand until it is too dry to hold together. Making things with wet sand is very appealing to children, and they will want to wet the sand again and again.

THOUGHTS ON INVESTIGATING SAND

Sand is a material found in almost all preschool settings. It is so common that you may take it for granted, but you should recognize the importance of sand as a learning tool for children.

PREPARING FOODS

Instead of offering ready-made snacks or step-by-step procedures to follow in making snacks, allow children to create their own snacks. By careful questioning, you can guide children to test their ideas about making foods that are good to eat. Some groups of children are more conventional than others in preparing foods. One group of three- and four-year-old children mixed sugar and butter with their oatmeal while another group chose peanut butter. Both groups said their snacks were delicious. Children have their own ideas about foods, and what they like to eat is not necessarily what adults like.

Science processes

Preparing foods requires children to make careful *observations* of the changes foods undergo. Children *predict* how foods will look, smell, feel, and taste. They make *inferences* based upon their cooking experiences such as "The vegetables are soft. They must have been cooked" and "It must be a fruit. It has seeds inside." *Time relations* are used as children decide how long foods should be cooked and in what order they should be prepared. *Classifying* and *comparing* skills are developed when foods are explored for likenesses and differences in smell, texture, size, and color. Children use *numbers* as they count the number of items they will need to prepare a food. Children *discuss* their discoveries about foods and draw *conclusions* such as "Some foods can be eaten raw" and "Foods can be baked or broiled in the oven and cooked on the stove."

What you need

Your choice of foods will be based on your budget and the prices of seasonal foods in your locality. Some nutritious foods that have been prepared successfully with children are

Green beans	Broccoli	Bread
Apples	Cauliflower	Carrots
Potatoes	Oatmeal	Eggs
Lettuce	Cheese	

Ingredients to be added to foods will vary with your budget, cooking facilities, and storage. Accompaniments for foods that have been used successfully are

Butter *or* margarine	Maple syrup	Nuts
Peanut butter	Cinnamon	Salt
Salad dressing	Pimento cheese	Raisins
Mayonnaise	Ketchup	Jelly

Cooking facilities will vary from classroom to classroom. The kind of facilities you have will determine your cooking activities to some extent. But you can substitute, for example, a potato masher for a blender, and most foods can be baked in a Dutch oven or cooked on a hot plate. There are foods such as apple salad, stuffed celery, and peanut butter that can be prepared without cooking. Suggested appliances and utensils include the following:

Refrigerator	Pots and pans	Dutch oven
Stove	Cooking utensils	Toaster oven
Hot plate	Eating utensils	Dishes

What you should consider

It should be clear that it is children who make the major decisions about investigating foods rather than you. There are, however, ideas that children may have that are impractical or unsafe. If children make suggestions such as building a fire to roast hot dogs or baking three cakes on the same day, it is your responsibility to explain why these suggestions are not feasible.

How you organize

If the children in your classroom are unaccustomed to preparing foods, you may want to choose several children to make the snack and assure the other children that they will have a turn another day. A list of names posted in the classroom helps children to understand when their turn will come. If the children in your classroom have had cooking experiences, it usually is not necessary to choose one group. Instead children who are interested and excited about cooking may come to the food center whenever they want to.

ACTIVITY 1
EXPERIMENTING WITH LETTUCE

What you need

Lettuce
Dishes
Eating utensils
Toppings children may want to put on lettuce (e.g., peanut butter, Cheeze Whiz, salad dressing)

How you begin

You may choose any nutritious food to introduce the first activity. Lettuce was found to be a suitable food for both nursery school and kindergarten children. Place a wrapped head of lettuce on a table where six to eight children are seated.

Predicting

Ask the children,

What kind of food is this?

In one nursery school seven children said, "Lettuce," and one child said, "Cabbage." The teacher asked, "How can we tell whether it's lettuce or cabbage?" The children answered, "Open it." When the wrapper was removed the children began to pull the leaves off the lettuce. The child who had said it was cabbage held up a leaf and said, "It's lettuce."

How you continue

Next you can ask,

Can we eat it like this?

In one class a child said, "We could cut it." The children preferred to cut the lettuce with table knives rather than tear the leaves. The children said the lettuce should be washed. They put it in two large bowls and took turns running water over it. Then the children chose the amount of lettuce they wanted to put in their bowls.

Observing

One child wanted his lettuce ground up in a blender. He put his lettuce and a little water in the blender and said, "Turn it on high." Later he said, "It looks like green slime!" This description did not bother him, the other children in the group, or the teacher, who all drank part or a full cup of the "green slime." One child said, "It's good. It tastes like water!" It was interesting that children who

had not prepared the snack did not want to taste the "green slime" at snack time.

Communicating

You should have on hand toppings your children like, and keep them where they cannot see them. When the lettuce is served, ask

> What would you like to put on your lettuce?

One teacher expected to hear the children say "dressing" and was surprised to hear the majority of the children say, "peanut butter." Some of the children preferred Cheese Whiz. A few children put all three toppings on their lettuce. The children *described* the snack as "good," "great," "delicious," and "neat!" There was enough lettuce for all the children to have snacks.

Using time relations

While the children eat their snack, you can encourage the development of *time relations* by asking,

> What did we do to the lettuce first? Second? Third?
> Does the lettuce look the same as it did before you put it in your cup?
> How has it changed?
> Is it still the same color?

How investigation continues

The children's enthusiasm and appetite for their snack will assure you that children like to plan their snacks and will eat what they prepare.

ACTIVITY 2
BOILING AND BAKING GREEN BEANS

What you need

Green beans
Plastic bag
Cooking pot
Baking pan
Timer
Dishes

Toppings children may want to
    put on beans
Stove or hot plate and toaster
    oven
Eating utensils

How you begin

To introduce the activity, place a plastic bag filled with green beans on a table. Ask the children,

> Can you tell me what is inside the bag?

Most children are familiar with beans and will quickly identify them. A few children may have only seen cut beans. One three-year-old said, "That's okra," and another child said, "They're baby cucumbers."

Observing

Ask the children to look at the beans carefully:

> What color are the beans?
> Take a bean from the bag and feel it. How does it feel? Hard? Soft?
> How does it smell?

Allow the children to wash and taste the beans. Some children will discover the seeds inside. Ask the children,

> How do the raw beans taste? How do they smell?

How you continue

Next ask the children how they would like to prepare the beans for snacks. One group of three- and four-year-old children suggested cooking the beans on the stove and in the oven. The teacher asked, "Is there anything we need to do before we cook the beans?" One child said, "We have to string the beans." The children thoroughly enjoyed this activity. No child suggested cutting or snapping the beans. After the beans were strung, the teacher asked, "What do we need to put in the pot with the beans? In the pan?" The children agreed that water should be put in the cooking pot and the baking pan.

Using time relations

In order to develop an awareness of *time relations* the teacher asked, "How long should the beans cook?" The children replied, "Ten minutes." The timer was set for ten minutes.

Predicting

You can encourage the children to *predict* what the beans would look like at the end of the cooking time.

> Will the beans be the same color?
> How do you think the beans will feel when you touch them? Will they be hot?
> Will they taste the same as they did before they were cooked?

Comparing

The teacher allowed the children to look at the beans on top of the stove and in the pan in the oven. They noticed that the water was boiling in both containers. At the end of ten minutes both containers of beans were removed from the stove. The teacher allowed the children to taste the beans. You can help children make *comparisons* (the first step in seriation) between the boiled and baked beans by asking,

> Do the beans look the same? Taste the same? Smell the same?
> Do we need to cook the beans longer?

The children in the class said: "The beans are still green." "They are darker green in the pan." "They taste O.K." "Let's eat them." If children disagree about the length of time the beans should cook, some beans can cook longer, and the others can be eaten right away.

How investigation continues

For snack the children had their choice of raw beans, cooked beans, or baked beans. A few children ate all three kinds of beans. The teacher asked the children what they wanted to put on their beans and all of the children said salt. One child opened each bean pod and then ate the seeds. Later he ate the bean pods. A child who did not help prepare the snack refused to eat the beans. He said, "I don't like beans—no way!" The teacher wondered if this child's attitude would have been different if he had helped prepare the beans for snack.

ACTIVITY 3
BAKING AND MASHING POTATOES

What you need

Potatoes   Butter *or* margarine
Peelers   Other toppings children may want to put on
Timer   potatoes
Dishes   Stove *or* hot plate and toaster oven
Blender   Eating utensils
Salt   Cooking pot

How you begin

Choose small baking potatoes for the snack. Show the potatoes to the children and ask,

What are these called?

Observing and communicating

Encourage discussion about the potatoes by asking,

What color are potatoes?
What color are they inside?
How do raw potatoes taste?

Cut a potato and give each child a small piece to taste. *Talk about* how potatoes look and taste. One group of five-year-olds described a raw potato as tasting "like water," "good," "like nothing," "bad," and "ugh." Ask the children,

How can we prepare the potatoes for a snack?

Children may have different answers such as bake, cook, mash, and fry. You should try to prepare the potatoes in as many different ways as the children suggest. Potatoes, or any food, can be prepared in more than one way on different days.

Using number

One group of five-year-old children chose to bake and to mash potatoes. They were able to peel the potatoes, cut them, and put them in a pot to cook. The children who wanted baked potatoes decided to eat one-half of a potatoe each. Six potatoes were put in the oven to bake for 15 minutes. When the timer went off, the children stuck a fork into the boiled and baked potatoes. They agreed the boiled potatoes were done, but that the baked potatoes needed to bake longer. The timer was set again to go off in 15 minutes. After 15 minutes the children tested the baked potatoes and decided they should bake 15 more minutes. One child said, "It took four 15's before our potatoes were done." Children experienced *number* relationships as they set the timer for 15 minutes and talked about eating one-half of a potato.

How investigation continues   The children who wanted mashed potatoes had their snack earlier. They watched the potatoes as they were whipped in a blender. Then the children served themselves potatoes. Foods they chose to stir into their mashed potatoes were butter, salt, cheese, and peanut butter. Toppings the other children chose for their baked potatoes were butter, sour cream, cheese, peanut butter, cottage cheese, and ketchup.

Concluding   Some *conclusions* children drew after several cooking experiences were: "Everybody doesn't like the same things to eat." "Foods can be cooked on top of the stove or baked in the oven." "It takes more time to cook some foods than others." "Children can think of ways to cook foods." "Foods made by children are good to eat."

ACTIVITY 4
DICTATING RECIPES

What you need

Chart paper
Index cards—5″ × 8″
Tag board pieces—5″ × 8″—*or* manila file folders cut in half
Felt-tip markers and/or crayons
Manila drawing paper
Colored construction paper
Stapler

How you begin

You can expect five-year-old children who are familiar with following the steps of recipes you have written on chart paper to have no difficulty dictating their cooking experiences.

Using number and time relations

The five-year-olds who baked potatoes in activity 3 made recipe cards. They told their teacher, one step at a time, what to write on large index cards. The recipe read:

Card 1 Wash three potatoes.
Card 2 Cut potatoes in half.
Card 3 Put the potatoes in the oven and bake at 350° for one hour.
Card 4 Put what you like to eat on the half potato.
Card 5 Eat the potato.

Then to illustrate each step, the children drew pictures on pieces of tag board. The index cards were attached to the pictures to make recipe cards. The children followed the recipe cards and baked potatoes for snacks again. The teacher also copied the recipe steps on a stencil and made mimeographed copies for the children to take home.

This experience involves *number* and *time relations* since children describe the order of events in preparing foods and the cards are numbered consecutively from 1 to 5. Some groups of four-year-old children are able to tell in sequential order how they prepared a food. They can dictate the steps as the teacher writes them down on chart paper or on cards. You will have to use your judgment about your children's ability to dictate events in sequential order.

Communicating Some <u>four-</u> and <u>five-year-olds</u> may want to make a book of their recipes, using manila drawing paper and a cover of colored construction paper.

ACTIVITY 5
PREPARING APPLES

What you need

Six apples
Chart paper
Stapler
Stencils
Dishes
Eating utensils

Other ingredients for snacks that children suggest
Other utensils and equipment to prepare snack children suggest
Crayons *or* pencils
Colored construction paper

How you begin

Give children an opportunity to prepare apples for snacks. A different group of six children can plan an apple snack each week for four or more weeks. Assure the children that every child will have a turn to prepare a snack.

Observing and communicating

Ask children to sit at a table with a bowl of six apples. Say to the children,

> What color are the apples?
> How many apples are in the bowl?
> Do they smell?
> How do they feel?

Encourage the children to *describe* the apples as they feel and smell them. Typically children describe apples as "pretty," "red," "green," "yellow," "two colors," "smell good," "hard," "round," "thick," and "big at the top and little at the bottom."

Classifying and comparing

Help the children to *classify* and *compare* the apples by asking,

> Are the apples the same?
> Are they the same color? Size?
> Do they smell alike?
> How are they different?

How you continue

Discuss with the children how they want to fix the apples for snack. Help them come to a decision; they may vote on the kind of snack if necessary. Follow the children's suggestions as closely as possible.

Using time relations

Tell the children to think of how to prepare the snack. Ask them,

What will we need to make the snack?
What is the first thing we should do? Second? Third?
What will we do next?

Write the children's directions on chart paper so that you
can refer to it as the snack is made. Place the necessary

ingredients and equipment on the table. Tell the children you are going to read the first sentence on the list, and then they should do what it says.

Predicting and inferring

While the children are making snacks, encourage them to make *predictions* by asking,

> What do you think our snack will look like after we add the _____?
> What color is it now?
> How do you think it will taste?

Allow the children to taste small portions of the snack after various ingredients are added. To help children make *inferences*, ask,

> Why do you think our snack is brown [color]? Is soft [hard, mushy, lumpy]? Smells good?
> What do you think would happen if we forgot _____ [ingredient or process]? Why?
> How would it taste? Why?

Using time relations and concluding

One group of six five-year-olds made Apple Fruit Mix. The first item on their list was, "Wash six apples and one orange," and the second, "Cut the apples in pieces and peel them." The children discovered that peeling small pieces of apple was difficult. They *concluded* that peeling a whole or half apple would be easier.

Using time relations and communicating

A class book of recipes can be made for the children to take home. Read and discuss the recipe with the children. Write each step on the top of a stencil, and ask different children to *draw* a picture of each step. Do this with each group that prepares an apple snack. Run the sheets off on a mimeograph machine. Put the ditto sheets between covers of colored construction paper, and staple the books. Give each child a book to take home.

The Apple Salad recipe made by the group of five-year-olds mentioned above was as follows:

1. Wash six apples and one orange.
2. Cut the apples in pieces and peel them.
3. Scoop out the orange with a spoon.
4. Add raisins.
5. Add sprinkles to the fruit.
6. Top with peanut butter, if you like.

An interesting recipe by a group of <u>four-year-olds</u> was for Apple Milkshake. It read as follows:

1. Get the blender, the ice cream, milk, and apples.
2. Cut up the apples, peel them, and put them in the blender.
3. Add ice cream (three spoonfuls) and a full cup of milk.
4. Turn the blender on and stir it up well.
5. Drink it.

How investigation continues

Throughout the year continue to prepare fruit for snacks. Suggestions of fruits are pears, lemons, oranges, peaches, and bananas. Children will discover that fruits prepared in many ways are good to eat.

THOUGHTS ON PREPARING FOODS

Preparing snacks can be a creative learning experience for children if you are willing to plan carefully and allow them to use their own ideas about foods. It may not be possible for the children to prepare their own snacks every day, but they should become actively involved in preparing foods as often as possible. There are many nutritious foods that the children and you can prepare together. I have found the above activities to be successful with <u>three-</u>, <u>four-</u> and <u>five-year-old</u> children.

SETTING OBJECTS
IN MOTION

Setting objects in motion is appealing to children because they can act on objects and immediately see the results of their actions. Children's excitement increases each time they are successful in moving an object. Through their experiences they learn more about the attributes of objects and find that there are many successful ways of setting them in motion.

Science processes

Activities can be introduced with a challenging question,

Can you find an object that you can blow across the table?

Children must *observe* carefully to discover which actions are most effective in moving objects. Similarities and differences between and among objects and the effects of various actions on them are discovered by children. After repeated experiences with setting objects in motion, objects may be *classified* as easy and hard to move and actions on objects as effective and ineffective. *Predictions* are made about the effectiveness of moving objects on different surfaces. Children *communicate* by sharing experiences verbally and/or by demonstrating what they have found out from their actions. *Inferences* are made when children give explanations based upon what they have observed: "Feathers are easy to move because they are light." "The bead moves fast because it is round." "The block is easy to move when you put it in a box and float it across the water." "The stone won't move by blowing on it. It's too heavy." *Space/time relations* are explored as children blow down on, at the side of, underneath, close to, and far away from objects.

What you need for motion activities

Jumbo straws
Variety of small objects, such as wooden blocks, Legos, pegs, crayons, Styrofoam pieces, feathers, pencils, wooden beads, Cuisenaire rods, unit blocks, cotton balls

ACTIVITY 1
BLOWING OBJECTS WITH STRAWS

What you need

Table
Jumbo straws
Variety of small objects

How you begin

Place some straws and a variety of small, familiar objects on a table. Good choices are a cotton ball, a crayon, a Styrofoam piece, a wooden bead, a small block, and a pencil. Have the children take a straw, then say,

> **Which object do you think you can move across the table by blowing through the straw?**

Have them try to do this. Notice which objects they choose and how well they succeed. If more than one group of children shows an interest in the activity, place duplicate objects on other tables.

Observing and inferring

Encourage *observation* by asking questions such as,

> **What happened when you blew on the cotton? The block? The crayon?**
> **Which object is easier to move?**
> **Why do you think the block is harder to move than the cotton?**

One nursery school child explained, "The cotton is soft, and the block is hard" and another child said, "The cotton is weak, and the block is strong." These *explanations* were logical, based upon the children's background of experience.

Communicating

Children may pick up an object and move it. You should accept this method of moving objects since it demonstrates a legitimate way to move them. Another way to move objects is with wheel toys. If children use this method, have them *talk about* the way wheels can help to move objects. Encourage children to experiment with objects that are round like wheels. Children will realize that a bead moves easily because "It's round," "It's a circle," "It's like a wheel." One four-year-old child commented that a crayon and a pencil rolled "round and round." When the teacher asked "Why," the child replied, "Because it's round. A flat crayon won't go round."

Predicting and inferring

Encourage children to choose objects in the classroom for exploration. Ask questions to encourage experimentation with the objects:

> What would happen if you blew on the object again?
> Why do you think it moved?
> Why do you think it didn't move?
> Can you think of another way to make it move?

During their explorations children may change the position of the objects. They may place crayons upright and beads on their sides. They will find that changes in position affect the motion of objects. Children may try to move several objects at the same time. One child stacked three blocks and tried to blow them down with a straw. When she didn't succeed, she began with the top block and blew each one down in succession.

115

ACTIVITY 2
EXPERIMENTING WITH CARDBOARD ROLLERS

What you need

Jumbo straws
Cardboard rollers from paper towels and/or toilet paper
Variety of small objects

How you begin

Ask the children to select some objects to try to move by blowing. Give the children straws and cardboard rollers to use in moving the objects.

Comparing

Encourage *comparisons* between the rollers and the straws:

> What happens when you blow through the roller?
> What happens when you blow through the straw?
> Does it make any difference which objects you try to move?

Children will discover that the rollers are not always more effective than the straws. One child said that a paper roller was too long to move a small rock. The teacher suggested cutting the roller to make it shorter. Several small pieces were used successfully to move the rock. Encourage the children to use long and short straws and rollers. Ask questions such as

> What happens when you use the short roller? The short straw? The long roller? The long straw?
> What happens when you blow on the top of the objects? The sides? Under the objects?

Communicating and classifying

Allow children to experiment with straws and cardboard rollers and objects as long as they are interested. Two five-year-olds built a door with three rollers. They found that blowing on any one of the rollers would knock all of them down. Some of the children enjoyed blowing objects through the rollers. They discovered that if several rollers were placed end-to-end it was difficult to blow objects through them. In order to succeed they had to place a straw inside the first roller. Some children will tape several straws or rollers together in an effort to move objects faster. They will find that this method isn't always more effective. Encourage children to *communicate* with each other by sharing ideas. Many children will act on their classmates' ideas and sometimes expand them. Children will begin to *classify* objects as "easy" or "hard to move" and methods of moving objects as "effective" and "ineffective."

ACTIVITY 3
BLOWING OBJECTS ON A RUG

What you need

Rug
Jumbo straws
Cardboard rollers
Variety of small objects

How you begin

Children may place objects on the rug during their first attempts to move objects. If they are still using the table, you can encourage them to try blowing objects that are placed on the rug. Children will find that it is more difficult to move objects on a rug than on a table top or a tile area.

Predicting

Help the children to make *predictions* by asking,

What will happen if you put the _____ on the rug? On the table? On the tile?

Choose an object you think will move on the tile. Will it move on the table? Will it move on the rug?

Inferring

To encourage making *inferences*, ask the children,

Why do you think objects move more easily on tile than on the rug?

Do they move more easily on the table or on the tile? Why do you think so?

Did objects move more easily on the rug when you blew through the straw or the roller? Why do you think so?

One three-year-old tried to blow a bead with his mouth. When the bead didn't move on the rug, he put it on the table and blew it. The bead moved right away, and the child said to his teacher, "It just works better on the table."

ACTIVITY 4
USING PAPER CONES

What you need

Construction paper
Masking tape
Variety of small objects

How you begin

Make construction paper cones with small and large openings. Encourage the children to blow through them in order to move objects.

Using spatial relations

Spatial relations can be experienced as children blow down and on various sides of an object. Ask questions to encourage children's explorations:

> What happens when you blow on the top of the object?
> Will it move if you blow on its side? Underneath?
> What happens when you blow through the big end? The small end?
> Will it move if you get closer? Move farther away?
> Why do you think so?

Children will discover that the position, distance from an object, and the stream of air make a difference in the movement of an object.

Classifying

Make available a variety of colored construction paper and tape. Have the children roll the paper to make a cone and then blow through it to move an object. Children will use both ends of the cones and discover that objects, for the most part, move more easily when air comes out of the small end. One child said, "The big end won't blow. Let's try the little one. It blows."

ACTIVITY 5
MOVING OBJECTS IN WATER

What you need

Water table *or* large transparent plastic container
Jumbo straws
Cardboard rollers from paper towels and/or toilet paper
Variety of small objects

How you begin

Fill the water table with water. Have the children choose an object and move it across the water. Some children will use the straws and rollers; others will move objects by making waves with their hands. You should limit the number of objects in the water since the moving objects have an effect on each other. To avoid long waits, several containers should be filled with water.

Observing

Events with the water table can be the most enjoyable and interesting to the children. They will discover new ways to make objects move. One four-year-old child found that she could make a rock move under the water by placing a straw near the rock and blowing lots of bubbles. Other discoveries children made were that floating objects move when the water moves, making waves with your hands moves objects, some objects sink when they get wet, blowing bubbles with straws or rollers moves objects, blowing hard with your mouth makes objects move, and objects can be moved by floating them in containers.

Classifying and communicating

Children will find it is easier to move some objects in water than it is to move them on other surfaces. They also find it easier to make objects move in water without blowing through tubes. One child stopped blowing through a straw and said, "I have to stop; my stomach is all out of air." Another child put water in a plastic egg, and said, "It won't move. My breath isn't strong enough." The teacher asked, "What would happen if you took the water out?" The child opened the egg, let the water out, and blew on it. The egg moved in the water, but a child who was watching said, "If you put water in the egg, and get a bunch of straws, and blow hard it will also move." He demonstrated his findings for the other children.

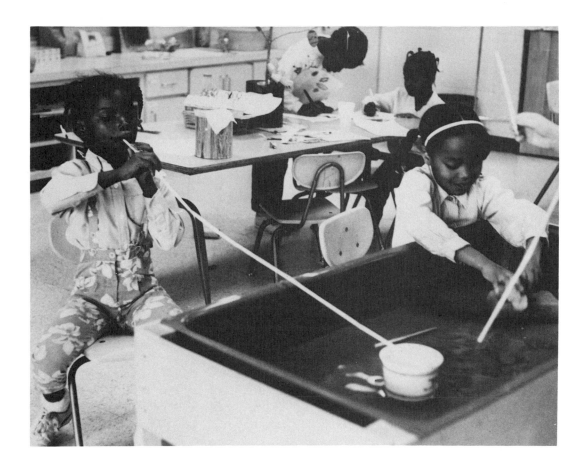

Inferring

Children may invent games with the objects. Two boys blew a block back and forth to each other. Several children raced their objects across the water table. You can ask questions to encourage experimentation:

How did you make the _____ move across the water?
Is there another way you can make it move?
Why do you think the _____ moved faster than the _____?
What happens when you put an object in water?
Does it move? Why? Why not?
How can you make it move?

Although children may see the same event taking place, they may not agree on the reason(s) why it happens. Children will give their own explanations for why something happens based upon their experiences.

ACTIVITY 6
MAKING OBJECTS MOVE

What you need

Water table *or* large, transparent plastic container
Aluminum foil
Construction paper
Finger paint paper
Newsprint
Clay
Fabric

How you begin

Give the children aluminum foil cut into different pieces. Ask them to make an object that they can move across the water table. Allow the children to choose the size of foil they want to use. Three- and four-year-old children may put a piece of foil in the water without changing its form. You can encourage making objects by asking questions such as

> Can you fold the foil?
> Can you fold the foil to make a rim on each side?

Five-year-olds usually make some kind of boat. A few may make cups, bird nests, or amphibious planes.

Observing

Children will enjoy successfully moving their objects across the water. Encourage experimentation by asking questions:

> How did you move your boat across the water?
> Does it move when you blow on it?
> Does it move when you make waves with your hands?
> What made your boat sink?
> Can you move objects across the water in your boat?

They will stay afloat unless water gets inside, heavy objects are placed in the boats, or the foil is rolled into a tight ball.

How investigation continues

Provide construction paper, finger paint paper, and newsprint for making other objects. Children will find these materials will tear and fall apart when they are wet. Encourage experimentation with other materials in the classroom. One group of five-year-olds made boats with clay and another group added cloth sails to their foil boats.

THOUGHTS ON SETTING OBJECTS IN MOTION

Children learn through experimentation that objects can be set in motion using a variety of methods. They begin to observe objects in motion and attempt to explain what causes the motion. Activities with wheels, springs, gears, and pulleys are appealing to children.

DISCOVERING SEEDS

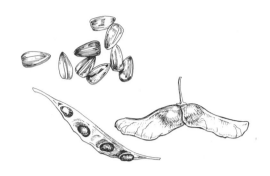

Children are attracted to seeds in all their forms. They find seeds on the ground and keep them as treasured possessions. They enjoy the variety of colors, sizes, and shapes of seeds. They use seeds to decorate their favorite mud pies and cakes. They enjoy watching seeds sprout and plants grow.

Science processes

Children *observe* seeds as they *classify* them according to size, shape, and color. Seriation skills are developed when children choose seeds for planting and *compare* the growth of plants. Children *predict* which seeds will sprout and how plants will grow. From their experiences with seeds children make *inferences* about the conditions necessary for growth. Children use *number* and *measurement* as they count seeds to be planted and estimate the growth of plants. Children draw *conclusions* from their experiences with seeds such as "Plants grow from seeds" and "Seeds do not all look alike."

What you need for seeds activities

You will need seeds that sprout easily. In the bean family this includes black-eyed peas, lentils, great northern beans, cranberry beans, pinto beans, butter beans, large lima beans, baby lima beans, and navy beans. Other seeds that sprout easily are

Corn	Marigold
Peas	Sunflower
Pumpkin	Apple
Radish	Grapefruit
Grass	Orange

ACTIVITY 1
EXAMINING BEANS

What you need

Three kinds of dried beans (e.g., pinto, lima, and navy)
Three large containers
Plastic *or* paper plates
Magnifying glasses

How you begin

Place bags of three different types of dried beans on a table. Choose beans that are as unlike as possible. Pinto beans, lima beans, and navy beans are good choices. Children will naturally gravitate to the bags of beans. Questions and comments children have made about beans are as follows: "What are those?" "Are we going to have them for snack?" "I've never seen beans like this before." "Those are lima beans." "Can we open the bags?" "Where did they come from?" Read the labels on the bags and allow the children to open the bags and place some of each kind of bean in three large containers. Give the children plates to fill with beans from the large containers.

Observing and communicating

Encourage the children to *observe* and *talk about* the beans:

> Do they look alike?
> Do they have any parts that are the same?
> Are they the same color? Size? Shape?
> How are they different?

Give the children magnifying glasses to use while they examine the beans. Comments made by three-, four-, and five-year-old children about beans were as follows: "The beans are hard." "They have funny places" (scars on bean seeds where they were attached to the pod). "They are too hard to peel." "These beans are white." "These beans have spots." "These beans look just alike." The purpose of examining the beans is not to name the parts, but to notice the likenesses and differences between and among beans.

126

ACTIVITY 2
NOTICING LIKENESSES AND DIFFERENCES IN SEEDS

What you need

Four kinds of dried beans
Three large containers
Variety of seeds from other vegetables—other beans, corn, radish
Variety of seeds from fruits—orange, apple, lemon, grape, peach

How you begin

Place the three containers each holding three kinds of bean seeds on a table. Add some of a fourth kind of bean seed to each container.

Classifying

Talk about the new seeds and how they are alike and different from the other seeds in the containers. Have the children choose a handful of bean seeds and put them on the table. Ask them to put the beans together that are alike in some way.

Most children will *classify* the beans by sorting them into like groups. Some children will *classify* by color and/or size. One five-year-old child said, "I put all the white beans together and all the brown beans together. What do I do about these?" The teacher asked, "Are they white or brown?" The child said, "They are white and brown." The teacher asked, "Are they alike?" The child said, "Yes, I'll put them in a group by themselves."

How investigation continues

Each day add a few more seeds to the containers. These may be different kinds of bean seeds and/or other seeds such as corn and radish. Encourage children to group the seeds as before. Several nursery school children put orange seeds from their snacks in the various containers. The children continued to save seeds from their snacks until they had added apple, lemon, grape, and peach seeds. Allow children to bring fruits from home, cut them open, and examine the seeds. Tell the children that the part of the plant containing seeds is called the fruit of the plant.

ACTIVITY 3
OPENING SEEDS

What you need

Lima bean seeds
Variety of other seeds such as other bean, corn, radish, grass, apple, cherry
Large containers
Magnifying glasses
Baby food jars

How you begin

Soak lima bean seeds overnight to soften them. Rinse the beans several times with water, and put them in large containers on a table. Allow the children to take some beans from the containers.

Observing and communicating

Encourage the children to open the beans and discover the baby plant, or embryo. Ask questions such as

> What do you see inside the bean seed?
> What does it look like?

Five-year-olds *described* the embryo as "a plant," "little beans," and "leaves and roots." Three- and four-year-old children talked about "the little leaves" inside the seeds. Give the children magnifying glasses and allow them to remove the embryo from the bean seed. Talk about the leaves and attached part that becomes the roots and stem. Tell the children the baby plant is called an embryo. Some children may want to plant the embryo in sand or soil. Allow them to plant and care for them as they would any seed. They will discover that the embryo will not grow without the rest of the bean seed.

How you continue

Most children will ask to soak other seeds in water. Encourage them to experiment with as many seeds as possible. Throughout the room in one kindergarten there were baby food jars filled with seeds soaking in water. The jars contained bean, corn, radish, grass, apple, and cherry seeds.

Inferring

Children will find baby plants in the bean and corn seeds. The other seeds are either too hard to open or too small to see the embryo. You can ask,

Can you find the embryo in the bean seeds? Corn seeds?
Why can't you see the embryo in the smaller seeds?

The children may answer, "The seeds are too hard to
open" and "The embryo is too little to see."

ACTIVITY 4
EXPERIMENTING WITH SEEDS

What you need

Variety of seeds
Sponges
Sand table
Sprinkling can
Paper towels
Two pieces of glass (3″ × 5″, 4″ × 4″, 5″ × 8″)—purchase from scientific supply house or hardware store; cover edges with masking tape

How you begin

By now some groups of children will have suggested planting seeds; other groups will choose to concentrate on examining seeds. Children may find seeds on the playground to add to their collection of seeds. You must be certain that the seeds children collect are not poisonous.

Observing

Acorns are especially appealing to children. In the fall children may collect quantities of acorns and in the spring pull up the young oak plants. The plants usually are growing from the acorn seeds and can readily be seen by the children. They provide an excellent example of the way plants grow from seeds. Children can also *observe* seeds sprouting by placing them on wet sponges. The roots will grow downward into the sponge and the stems upward. Seeds also may be placed between a wet paper towel and two pieces of glass. Sponges and towels must be kept wet. Most groups of children, however, ask to plant their seeds "in dirt."

Inferring

A situation such as the following may develop with the children in your class. In one nursery school the children wanted to plant seeds on the first day they were given seeds to examine. After talking about bean seeds, a four-year-old child said, "We have to plant these seeds right away. Let's get started." Another child said, "We can plant them in the sand table." The teacher didn't interfere with the children's plans. The children put seeds in the sand, poured water on them, and flooded the sand box. One child said, "There's lots of water to make them grow." The children looked for plants every day and sometimes pulled up the seeds to find out if they had sprouted. They continued to water the seeds. In a few days the sand table began

to smell. The children complained about the odor: "It smells because our plants are growing." "Something stinks." "The water looks funny." "The seeds are spoiled. Let's throw them away." When the seeds were examined, they smelled and fell apart in the children's hands. The contents of the sand table were discarded. In a similar situation you can encourage the children to make *inferences* about the seeds by asking,

> Why do you think the sand table smelled?
> Why do you think the seeds were rotten?

Most of the children said, "We put too much water on the seeds" and "The sand table had too much water."

How investigation continues You can suggest planting seeds again and giving them less water. In that class the seeds were planted, the sand sprinkled with water, and a little water added each day. To the delight of the children, bean plants appeared. It is important that the children have success in growing plants.

131

ACTIVITY 5
PLANTING SEEDS

What you need

Variety of easily sprouting seeds
Containers such as clay pots, baby food jars, *or* Styrofoam, plastic, or paper cups
Soil *or* sand from the playground, but potting soil may be used
Watering can
Popsicle sticks
Glue
Trowels *or* spoons

How you begin

Children should be allowed to choose the kind of seeds and as many seeds as they want to plant. As long as beans and corn seeds are watered, they will sprout even when they are planted deeply under the soil. Radish and grass seeds sprout overnight. It is desirable to gather soil and/or sand from outside rather than to use potting soil. If this is impossible, potting soil may be used. Children can plant seeds in any kind of small container. Encourage them to think about how they want to plant seeds by asking questions such as

What will you need to plant the seeds?
What kind of seeds will you plant?
How many seeds will you plant?
Where will you put the seeds after they are planted?

Allow children to choose their containers, seeds, and soil.

Using number

Most children will choose one to three seeds to plant; a few may select as many as six seeds. Some children will put seeds on the bottom or surface of the soil; others will make holes with their fingers, drop the seeds in the holes, and cover them with dirt. Encourage the children to *count* the seeds as they put them in the containers. Write the number and type of seeds on a slip of paper and glue it to one end of a Popsicle stick. Insert the other end in the container of the soil. Five-year-old children will usually water their seeds regularly, but three- and four-year-olds may forget to water theirs. A few children may lose interest in seeds entirely.

Predicting and inferring

Encourage children to make *predictions* about seeds that will sprout and the kinds of plants that will grow. When seeds sprout or do not sprout, help children to make *inferences* to explain what has happened by commenting and asking questions such as

> I see two plants growing in your container. What color are they?
> How many seeds did you plant?
> Why do you think one seed sprouted and the other one didn't?
> Let's look at the seed and find out why it didn't sprout.
> Can you show me how tall your plant has grown?
> How many leaves does your plant have?

Explanations given by five-year-old children about their seeds were as follows: "My seeds were too hard to sprout." "I forget to water them." "I gave them too much water. They rotted." "I planted them deep." "I planted too many seeds in one container." "They grew 'cause I watered them every day." "Bean seeds grow." "I put them in a sunny place." Three- and four-year-olds' explanations were less sophisticated: "They didn't want to grow." "I forgot to water them." "They were too little to grow." "I watered them." "I took good care of them."

ACTIVITY 6
DESCRIBING GROWTH

What you need

Dowels of various lengths
Strips of paper
Yarn
String

How you begin

You must be sure that every child has one or more seeds that sprout and grow into plants. A few younger children will remember which containers they planted seeds in by where they placed them in the room; others will suggest labeling the containers with their names. Most kindergarten children will suggest labeling their containers with their names and the types of seeds planted.

Observing and communicating

Children enjoy *observing* and *describing* their plants. They may indicate the growth of a plant with their hands. Holding his hands apart one child said, "My plant is this tall." This was an estimation of the plant's height rather than an exact measurement. Encourage children to estimate the changes in their plants' growth by asking questions such as

> How tall is your plant?
> Is it taller than the _____ plant?
> How do you know your plant has grown?
> How much has your plant grown?

Measuring

Provide children with several dowels of various lengths. Ask the children,

> Can you think of a way to use the sticks to measure your plant?

Most children will place a dowel beside a plant to estimate its height. Encourage the children to choose the dowel closest to the height of the plants by asking questions such as

> Can you find a stick that is almost as tall as your plant?
> Is the stick shorter than the plant? Longer than the plant?

Give children strips of paper, yarn, and string to *measure* their plants. Children may devise their own means of measurement. One four-year-old used his index finger to record the daily height of his plants. He drew a line on his

134

finger to indicate the top of the plant. He had difficulty recording the growth of the plant since the ink from the previous day was gone the following morning. His teacher suggested that he use strips of paper to measure the height of his plant. Each day he measured the plant and glued the strip of paper on construction paper. The result was a record of the growth of the plant.

Comparing

Several kindergarten children *compared* the growth of the class's bean and corn plants. Each time they observed a change in one or both plants they drew pictures to indicate the change(s). They kept a record of the plants' growth for 21 days. Two nursery school children placed their corn plants side by side to determine which one was taller. Three children compared their corn plants and found the tallest and shortest plant.

How investigation continues

Plants may be kept in the classroom for long periods of time if they are repotted from time to time. In one classroom children raised beans and grew new plants from their bean seeds.

THOUGHTS ON DISCOVERING SEEDS

Children are always fascinated by seeds. Seeds can be explored in so many ways that children seldom tire of playing with them. They enjoy seeds for their variety, smallness, and uses.

BUILDING STRUCTURES WITH BOXES

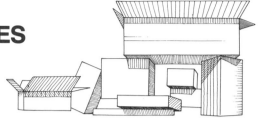

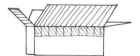

Building with boxes has the same fascination for children as building with blocks. Boxes are lighter than blocks. They come in many sizes and shapes. They are inexpensive and easily obtainable. They may be used indoors or outdoors. They are suitable for building any kind of construction. Children can easily modify a building by a shift in position, replacement, exchange, removal, or addition of boxes.

Science processes

Children learn the attributes of boxes by sorting them (*classification*) into various sizes and shapes and by discovering which ones are effective and ineffective in creating various structures. Skills essential to seriation are developed as children *compare* boxes and reject and accept them to use in particular structures. Through careful *observation* they learn which boxes are needed to complete or modify a structure. *Measurement* is used to determine which boxes are the same size and to estimate the height, length, and width of a structure. *Number* is used to find out how many boxes were used in building a structure and how many are needed to create a new structure. *Space/time relations* are involved when boxes are arranged and rearranged and the required distances between and among them determined. *Predictions* are made as children consider how many and what types of boxes can be added or taken away from a structure to complete it satisfactorily. Events are anticipated as children draw pictures of future constructions. Children *communicate* through their pictures and verbal descriptions of their structures. From the experimentation with box structures children make *inferences* about suitable and unsuitable choices for future constructions.

What you need for boxes activities	Variety of cardboard boxes such as shoe boxes, grocery food boxes, milk cartons, hat boxes, clothes boxes, flower boxes, office supplies boxes, Pringle potato chip cardboard cans, and any cylindrical-shaped boxes Newspapers Masking tape
How you prepare	Fill cardboard boxes of a variety of sizes with newspapers and tape them shut. This will make boxes firm and allow children to use them to build structures. Boxes should be light so that there is no danger of children being hurt by a falling box. You should prepare as many boxes as possible for children. A few different boxes added each day increase children's interest and motivate them to build new structures. Building with boxes can occur outdoors or indoors if space permits. One group of children built structures on the playground and indoors in the nap room when it wasn't in use. Furniture can be moved against the walls of a classroom and the space used for building.

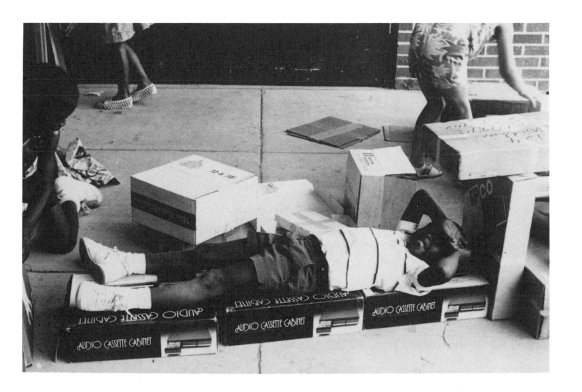

ACTIVITY 1
INTRODUCING BOXES

What you need

Variety of boxes filled with newspaper and taped shut
    Large, medium, and small
    Rectangular and square

How you begin

To introduce building structures, you should choose an assortment of large, medium, and small rectangular and square boxes that you have filled with newspaper and taped shut.

Inferring

Say to the children,

> Here is a group of boxes that have been taped shut. Do you think there is anything inside the boxes?

One five-year-old child said, "There's tape on the boxes to make you think there is something inside," and another child said, "There's a surprise inside." Open a few of the boxes and show the children the paper inside. Encourage the children to make *inferences* by asking,

> Why do you think I put papers in the boxes and taped them shut?

Children in one kindergarten answered: "To make the boxes hard." "So we can build with them." " 'Cause they will squash without the paper."

Observing

Tell the children that the papers make the boxes firm or hard so they can use them to build structures. Encourage careful *observation* by asking the children,

> What shapes are the boxes?
> Can you find a rectangle? A square?
> Do you see any other shapes?
> What sizes are the boxes?

Discuss the various shapes and sizes.

Classifying

Encourage the use of *classification* skills by saying,

> Put all the boxes that are alike in some way together.

The children will probably put like shapes together. Accept and discuss any classification systems the children choose.

138

Predicting

Encourage making *predictions* by asking:

What could you build with the square boxes? The rectangular boxes? The square and rectangular boxes? The small boxes? The large boxes?

<u>Five-year-olds</u> in one kindergarten talked about building houses, castles, towers, windows, and furniture. <u>Three-</u> and <u>four-year-old</u> children mentioned bridges, roads, houses, and garages.

ACTIVITY 2
BUILDING TALL STRUCTURES

What you need

Variety of boxes filled with newspaper and taped shut
    Large, medium, and small
    Rectangular and square
    Round and cylindrical

How you begin

Give the children the boxes used in activity 1. Encourage children to build tall structures with the boxes by asking questions such as

> Can you make a building that is taller than you are tall?
> Can you build a structure that is tall and won't fall down?

One group of five-year-olds built towers and then houses. Two three-year-old children built a condominium to live in at the beach. Several nursery school children built walls to throw balls over.

Measuring and using number

A few kindergarten children *measured* their towers by standing beside them. You can ask,

> Is the tower as tall as you are tall? How do you know?
> How much taller is it than you are? How much smaller?
> What can you do to make it as tall as you are? Taller?

One five-year-old said, "My tower is one box taller than I am," and another child said, "I need more boxes to make my tower taller than me. Help me, teacher." The teacher placed two boxes on top of the tower and asked, "If you wanted to build this tower again, how could you remember how tall it is?" He answered, "It's two boxes taller than me." The teacher asked, "Are the boxes the same size?" "No," he said, "one is fat and one is thin." The teacher asked, "How can you tell your friends how tall your tower is?" He replied, "One fat and one skinny box taller than me."

Encourage children to think about the height of their structures by asking questions such as

> How can you make your structure taller?
> How can you remember how tall it is?

Children will describe the height of their structures in different ways. One kindergarten child *measured* his structure with a piece of string, several nursery school children counted the *number* of blocks in their structures, and another child pointed to the teacher and said, "It's as tall as you are."

Comparing

In one nursery school children became interested in building tall walls. A girl attempted to throw a ball over her wall, but the ball hit the wall and knocked it down. She said, "I will build it taller than before and not use the small boxes, only big boxes, and it won't fall down again." When a boy's wall started to fall, he said, "I need fullest boxes (bigger)." Another boy's wall fell, and the teacher asked, "What can you do to keep your wall from falling down?" He said, "I'll make it stronger." He took his wall down and rebuilt it. This time he used a double row of boxes. The teacher asked, "Do you have the same number of boxes you had before?" The child answered, "Yes, but they are different." The teacher asked, "How are they different?" The child replied, "There are two stacks."

Observing

The five-year-olds decided to put windows in their towers which became houses. They placed two identical boxes upright and attempted to place the same kind of box across the top. The boxes fell down, and the children tried the same arrangement again. The teacher asked, "Can you find a long box that will fit across the top?" The children found a longer box that completed the window. After the window was in place, they were able to continue building their house by placing boxes around the window.

How investigation continues

Encourage children to continue building tall structures by introducing a few different boxes each day. If round or cylindrical boxes are available, provide these for the children. One nursery school child used Pringle cans for the chimney of his house, and another child used them to build a tower. She put two cans without lids on the bottom and when she put the last can on top, the tower fell. She solved the problem by putting the cans with lids on the bottom. When a child walked close to her structure, she said, "Don't breathe."

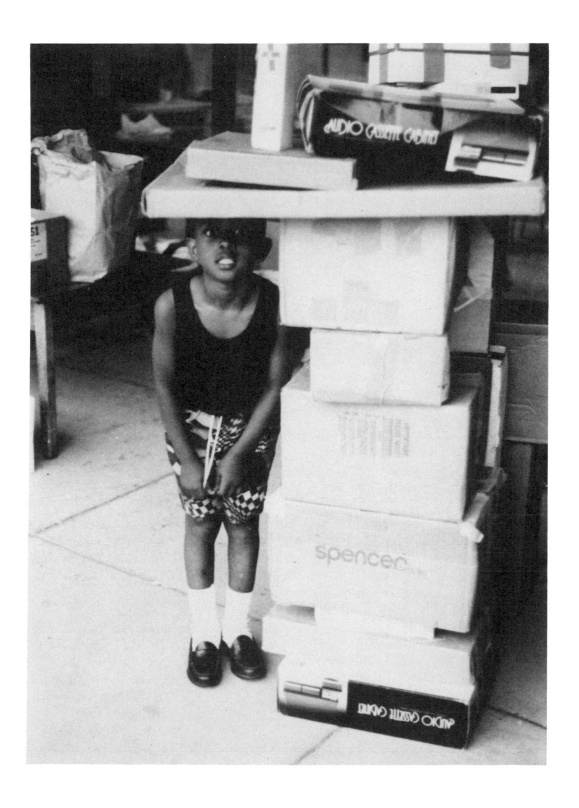

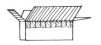

ACTIVITY 3
MAKING LONG STRUCTURES

What you need

Variety of boxes filled with newspaper and taped shut
    Large, medium, and small
    Rectangular and square
    Round and cylindrical

How you begin

Give the children the same boxes as in activity 2 and include several new ones. Ask the children,

> Can you think of something that is long to build with the blocks?

Using number and comparing

In one school several <u>five-year-olds</u> decided to make beds to sleep on. They lay on the floor and asked the teacher to place boxes beside them so they could tell how many they needed. In a similar situation, you could ask,

> How long are you when I use the big boxes? The small boxes?
> If I turn the rectangular boxes on their sides, will I need the same number of boxes?

The children *compared* the number of boxes needed in one circumstance with the number needed in another case. Soon they were able to estimate the *number* of boxes they would need to make beds, chairs, and tables.

Comparing and measuring

In one nursery school several children built bridges for cars to go under. One child said, "They are sharks in the water," and another child said, "We need a road built so cars can go over the bridge." She used boxes to build a square-shaped road connecting the bridge. She chose all big boxes to build the road, and when she ran out of boxes, the teacher asked, "Can you use the smaller boxes to complete the road?" She answered, "Yes," and combined the smaller boxes to make them even with the big boxes. This child *compared* the small boxes carefully and chose only those that when combined *equaled* the length and width of the big boxes.

Predicting

Two children became involved in building a house with a connecting tunnel. They told the teacher, "We need lots of boxes to make a long tunnel." The teacher provided more boxes and the children built walls. Then they put

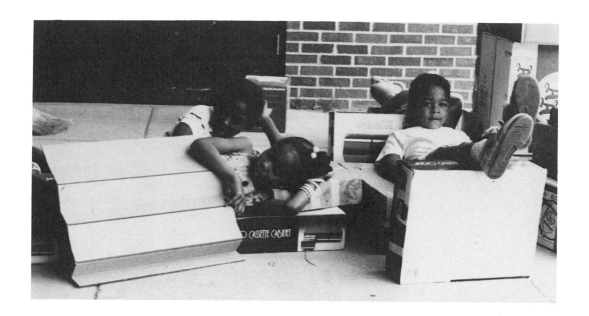

longer boxes on top of the walls so the tunnel would be dark. One child was building a road nearby and decided to make it longer so it would connect with the tunnel.

Using spatial relations

In another nursery school the teacher was surprised when two boys, three- and four-years-old, said they were going to build a bowling alley. The boys stacked a few boxes for a back wall and then stacked boxes along each side of the back wall to make side walls. Then they laid boxes flat on the ground between the walls and said, "This is the floor." They left a gap between the floor and the back wall. They said, "When we roll the ball, it will go into the hole." The children got a ball and rolled it into the hole. The teacher asked, "What would happen if you made the floor longer?" One boy said, "The ball would go farther." The boys found more boxes and made the floor longer and wider so it extended beyond the side walls. They moved the back and side walls to adapt to the floor. The teacher asked, "Why did you make the floor wider?" One child said, "So we'd have more room to stand."

How investigation continues

Encourage children to continue building as long as they are interested. Provide a few new boxes each day to motivate them to try building different structures.

ACTIVITY 4
USING STRUCTURES IN DRAMATIC PLAY

What you need

Variety of boxes filled with newspaper and taped shut
   Large, medium, and small
   Rectangular and square
   Round and cylindrical

How you begin

Provide the children with an assortment of boxes including a few new ones. As box building progresses, children's structures become more complex and show greater diversity. One child used the boxes to build a castle. He laid the big boxes down and said, "It is the porch." He started building boxes around him and then told the teacher, "You build the boxes around me, because I am a king in a castle."

Using spatial relations and communicating

Two children became involved in building houses. Their behaviors were very different from each other. Jim started with a definite plan as to how to build his house. He often named every box. Each one stood for something in the house, including the cat's milk and the dog's food. He often encouraged others to help him build; however, they had to follow his plan. If they used a box in a way he had not intended, he became upset and told them he didn't need that in his house. He seemed frustrated that they weren't "seeing" the same plan he was. Jim also turned boxes on their sides so that he covered the greatest amount of space possible. Ann, in contrast with Jim, encouraged others to build with her but did not stifle their ideas. It was as if she was building part of the house and they were adding to it. Ann did not turn boxes on their sides. At this point the teacher asked Ann if she could make the box take up more space on the floor? Ann looked at the box and said "No." She continued to build with the boxes turned straight up.

Using number and communicating

In one kindergarten two children built stairs going up and down to their house. The teacher asked, "How many boxes did it take to build the stairs?" "Two up and two down," the children answered. Boxes were used to divide the house into rooms. The teacher asked, "How do you know

146

where your rooms are?" One child pointed to the boxes and said, "We made the walls with the boxes." The children also made a playground with a fence around it. The teacher said, "Building a fence is a good idea. How many boxes did you use?" "Ten," said one child, "the playground is for my little girl." The children built chairs and beds with the boxes. One child got in bed, closed her eyes, and pretended to be asleep. Another picked up a paper bag and filled it with little boxes. She said, "I'm picking up the trash."

How investigation continues Sociodramatic play is a powerful motivation for children. With teacher guidance it can provide opportunities to stimulate their interest in and motivation for building structures with boxes.

ACTIVITY 5
DRAWING BUILDING PLANS

What you need

Variety of boxes filled with newspaper and taped shut
    Large, medium, and small
    Rectangular and square
    Round and cylindrical
Manila drawing paper
Felt-tip markers and/or crayons

How you begin

After students have been building structures with boxes for several days and verbally stating their ideas about what they are going to build, encourage them to try drawing building plans.

Using spatial relations and communicating

You can say to the children,

> Can you draw a picture of a house you want to make with boxes?

In one kindergarten several children *drew* pictures of the houses they planned to build. It was interesting that all the children drew front views of their houses. The children's constructions closely resembled their drawings. You can also ask,

> Can you draw pictures of the furniture you want for your houses?

Four children drew pictures of desks they planned to make with the boxes. Each child's drawings and constructions were different from the other children's. Some children drew beds, chairs, and tables. Their constructions also bore a close resemblance to their drawings. These four- and five-year-old children were able to use *spatial relations* to plan on paper what their structures would look like and build structures that closely resembled their plans.

THOUGHTS ON BUILDING STRUCTURES WITH BOXES

Teacher guidance is crucial if children are to receive maximum benefit from building structures with boxes. The kind of teacher guidance will be determined, to some extent, by the structures children build. Children's structures will vary with their age and background of experiences.

148

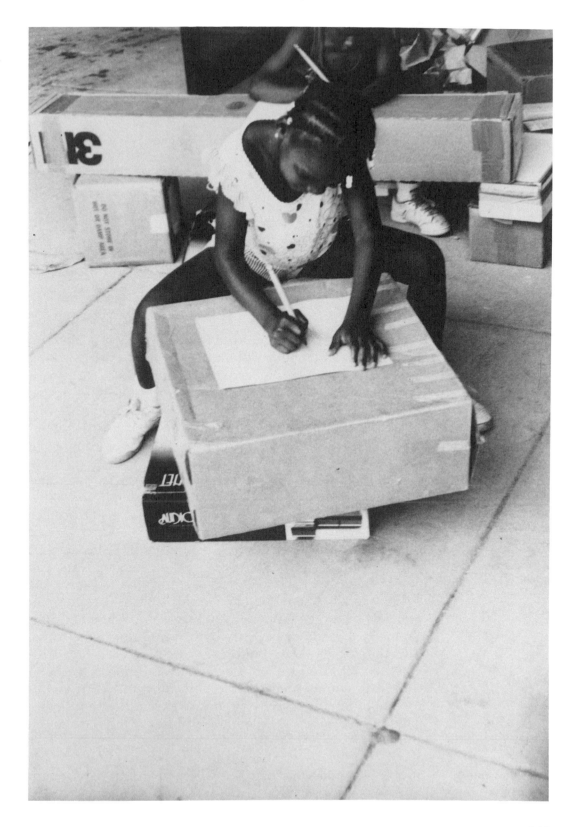

BLOWING BUBBLES

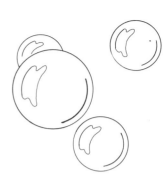

Blowing bubbles is an activity that is loved by all children. They can be exposed to a variety of bubble blowing adventures that involve them in the processes of science. Your guidance is invaluable in helping children to discover the relationships between their actions on bubbles and the effects of their actions.

Science processes

Careful *observation* is required by children to see the size, shape, color, and motion of bubbles. Children discover that bubbles do not always behave in the same way. They learn to make *comparisons* (essential for seriation) and notice and describe similarities between and among bubbles (essential for *classification*). They use *number* as they count bubbles and how many cans and straws were used to make them. They make *predictions* about the results of their actions on bubbles and *inferences* based upon what they find out. They *communicate* their findings through verbalizations and demonstrations of what they have discovered.

How you prepare

Most three-year-old children have blown bubbles and are familiar with blowing air out rather than sucking it in. You may need to help a few children learn how to blow. Ask children to practice blowing materials such as cotton, small pieces of paper, cellophane, and macaroni. When children can move these objects easily by blowing through a straw, they are ready to blow bubbles.

Often children's experiences with bubbles have been limited to commercial bubble solutions and equipment. For the following activities, you will want to use a homemade bubble solution. Allow the children to help make the solution.

What you need for bubble activities

Bubble solution—one part Ivory Liquid to four parts water. Add more soap if necessary. Glycerin may be added but is not necessary.

Low, transparent (if possible) plastic containers (about 15″ × 13″ × 7″) *or* plastic dishpans to hold the bubble solution

Low tables, blocks, *or* boxes outdoors on which to place the containers

ACTIVITY 1
BLOWING WITH JUMBO STRAWS

What you need

Bubble solution
Plastic containers
Tables, blocks, *or* boxes
Jumbo straws—several per child
Wastepaper basket

How you begin

Place several plastic containers filled with bubble solution on tables, blocks, or boxes outdoors. Near the containers place jumbo straws on a tray and the wastepaper basket for the used straws. Say to the children,

Can you blow bubbles with the straws and soapy water?

Blowing bubbles appeals so strongly to children that they will begin at once and may continue blowing bubbles for 30 minutes to an hour. Children become excited by the small bubbles they blow using straws. At first they may blow fast and hard to make "lots of bubbles." They soon discover that this method is unsatisfactory. They may not, however, associate blowing hard with a few or no bubbles. Allow children to experiment with blowing bubbles and to watch other children blowing bubbles. If children become frustrated by their inability to blow bubbles, ask,

What would happen if you blew slowly?

By blowing bubbles slowly children will see little bubbles coming out of the end of the straws.

Observing

Some bubbles pop as quickly as they are formed; others land on objects and can be seen for several seconds before they pop. One three-year-old squealed when a bubble slid down her straw to wet her hand: "Look at my bubble! It's on my hand." Then, disappointed, she said, "It popped." Allow the children to chase and pop their bubbles. Then try to get them to watch the bubbles until they pop. Make comments to encourage children to *observe* bubbles:

Let's watch the bubble and see where it goes. The bubble is on the grass. How long do you think it will be before it pops? Count with me. There is another bubble on a tree leaf.

Children will make observations about bubbles that are often overlooked by adults: "My bubbles ran together and popped." "I blew two bubbles. They are stuck together on my straw."

Comparing and classifying

Encourage children to notice *similarities* and *differences* among bubbles by asking questions such as

Did you blow one bubble? More than one bubble?
Were the bubbles big or little? Were they the same size?
Did the bubbles pop? Do you see any bubbles that haven't popped? Let's watch them.
How did you blow that bubble?
What shape are the bubbles? Are they all the same shape?
What color are the bubbles?

Observing

Most children agree that bubbles are round. They may have different opinions about their color. One three-year-old said, "Bubbles are white." A five-year-old said, "Bubbles don't have any color." Her classmates didn't all agree with her: "Bubbles are red and blue." "Bubbles are lots of colors. They look like rainbows." Children's *observations* about bubbles will depend upon their age and continued experimentation with bubbles. After blowing bubbles for several days, a group of four- and five-year-olds made the following observations: "Bubbles are different sizes." "Some bubbles look different when they land. They are flat on the bottom." "If you hold two straws together, you can blow bubbles." "Bubbles have pretty colors like the rainbow." "Bubbles stick to something wet." "Bubbles can go up in the air."

ACTIVITY 2
INTRODUCING FLEXIBLE STRAWS

What you need

Bubble solution
Plastic containers
Tables, blocks, *or* boxes
Jumbo straws—several per child
Flexible straws—several per child
Masking tape
Wastepaper basket

How you begin

Provide children with bubble solution, jumbo straws, and flexible straws. Children can continue experimentation with the jumbo straws and begin to explore blowing bubbles with the flexible straws. They will discover that the flexible straws bend at one end. Encourage experimentation with the straws by asking questions such as

> Can you blow bubbles through the bent end of the straw?
> When the bent end is up? Down?
> Can you blow bubbles through the long end of the straw?
> When the long end is up? Down?
> Why do you think you can blow bubbles with a bent straw?

Predicting

Most children will *predict* that bubbles can be made when the flexible end of the straw is turned down but not up. Ask children to blow through a flexible straw and feel the air on their hands when the flexible end is up and down. One five-year-old child said, "The air turns the corner." A three-year-old child said, "It's like magic."

Observing

Children may try to hold straws together with their hands to make "very long straws." Help children by taping jumbo and flexible straws together with masking tape. Attractive open designs can be made with the flexible straws. Sometimes children are surprised when bubbles come out of the ends of their interesting designs. One four-year-old said, "Look at my bubbles. They went up the straw and then down." Children will *observe* that when the end of a flexible straw is up, the bubbles will go up and then down. When the end of a flexible straw is down, the bubbles will go down. When the wind is blowing, however, bubbles may be carried up high and in any direction.

Comparing

Children may notice that the flexible straws blow bubbles slightly bigger than the jumbo straws. Ask the children,

> Why do you think the bubbles look bigger?
> Are the openings on the ends of the flexible straws larger than the openings on the ends of the jumbo straws?
> Does putting several straws together make the bubbles bigger?

Predicting

By now children probably have discovered that they can blow bubbles directly in the bubble solution. Most children will experiment and discover that a wet straw can be placed inside a bubble without its breaking. Encourage children to make *predictions* by asking,

> What do you think will happen if you put your straw inside the bubble?
> What will happen if you stop blowing?
> What will happen if you continue to blow?

Children will see that bubbles become larger as more air is blown into them. They begin to understand that more air means larger bubbles.

ACTIVITY 3
EXPERIMENTING WITH CANS AND ROLLERS

What you need

Bubble solution
Plastic containers
Tables, blocks, *or* boxes
Individual small juice cans—at least two dozen (Remove both ends. Smooth any sharp edges with a hammer or pliers.)
Assortment of fruit and/or vegetable cans—at least one dozen (Remove both ends. Smooth any sharp edges with a hammer or pliers.)
Cardboard rollers from paper towels and/or toilet paper
Masking tape
Wastepaper basket

How you begin

Provide children with bubble solution, cardboard rollers, juice cans, and an assortment of larger cans.

Comparing

Encourage children to try using the cans and rollers by asking questions such as

> Can you blow bubbles with the rollers and cans?
> Do you think the bubbles will be the same size as the bubbles you blew with the straws?

Children will discover that the rollers and cans have larger openings than the straws and make larger bubbles.

Observing

When the wind blows, children will be able to *observe* what happens to their larger bubbles. One group of five-year-old children observed several bubbles go over their school building. They ran to the other side of the building but couldn't find the bubbles. The children decided that the bubbles had popped before they hit the ground. Children enjoy watching and chasing bubbles as the wind carries them away. Occasionally they are successful in catching a bubble.

Predicting and inferring

Children soon learn that the cardboard rollers disintegrate in the water and discard them for the cans. If children don't succeed in blowing bubbles with the larger cans, they may discover that moving these cans in the air produces bubbles. You can help the children by asking,

Why can't you blow bubbles with the big cans?
What will happen if you move the cans in the air?

Using number

Help children to tape the juice cans together. As the children experiment, ask,

How many cans do you have taped together?
Are the bubbles bigger when you use two cans? Three cans? Four cans?

Observing

Encourage the children to *notice* colors in the bubbles by asking,

What colors do you see in the bubbles?
Do you see the same colors in all the bubbles?

Children will see rainbow colors in the bubbles as long as there is light indoors or outdoors. They may notice that the colors appear brighter on a sunny day.

Predicting

Jim, a four-year-old, said, "I am going to make red bubbles." He put red food coloring in the bubble solution and dipped a juice can in the mixture. He blew bubbles and said, "Look at my red bubbles." The other children said, "They aren't red." Then Jim put red tempera paint in the red solution. He blew several bubbles and exclaimed, "I'm making more red bubbles." The children became annoyed and said loudly, "No, you are not!" Jim appealed to the teacher for support and asked, "Aren't I making red bubbles?" She replied that she would get the stand-up mirror and he could look at his bubbles. Jim was disappointed when he looked in the mirror and saw that the bubbles weren't red. He said, "Well, I can make lots of bubbles. Watch and I'll show you." He ran to the water table, picked up a sieve, and dipped it in the bubble solution. He blew into the sieve and lots of bubbles came out. Jim said, "See, I told you I could make lots of bubbles." Jim had failed to make red bubbles, but he had found a way to make lots of bubbles.

ACTIVITY 4
USING SIEVES AND COLANDERS

**What you
need**

Bubble solution
Plastic containers
Tables, blocks, *or* boxes
Sieves with large holes
Colanders
Plastic objects with holes, if available

**How you
begin**

Give children bubble solution and a variety of sieves, colanders, and plastic objects with holes. Say to them,

Can you blow bubbles with the sieves? The colanders?

Comparing

Encourage children to make *comparisons* between bubbles from the sieves and from the colanders by asking,

**Are the bubbles from the sieves and from the colanders the
same size? Shape? Color?**

Children are fascinated with the variety of bubbles they
are able to blow with the sieves and colanders. They can
also move them through the air to make bubbles.

Inferring

Help children to make *inferences* from their experiences
by asking,

Why do you think the bubbles are small? Big?
Why does the colander make bigger bubbles than the sieve?
**Which sieve do you think made these bubbles? Which
colander?**

ACTIVITY 5
EXPLORING PIPE CLEANERS

What you need

Bubble solution
Plastic containers
Tables, block, *or* boxes
Pipe cleaners

How you begin

Give children bubble solution and pipe cleaners. Tell them to bend the pipe cleaners into any shape they like.

Predicting

Tell them they will use the pipe cleaners to blow bubbles. Encourage them to make *predictions* by asking,

What shape do you think the bubbles will be?

Most children predict that the bubbles will be the same shape as the pipe cleaners. They are surprised to see that the bubbles are round.

Inferring

Encourage experimentation with pipe cleaners by asking,

What shape are your bubbles?
Can you change the shape of your bubbles?
How do you think you can change their shape?
Is the bubble the same shape as the pipe cleaner?
What shape are the bubbles that the children are making?
Why do you think they are round?

Three-year-old children may say, "They like to be round." Five-year-old children may say, "Because all bubbles are round." Accept the children's answers since the explanations are logical to them and they do not have the background or experience to answer otherwise.

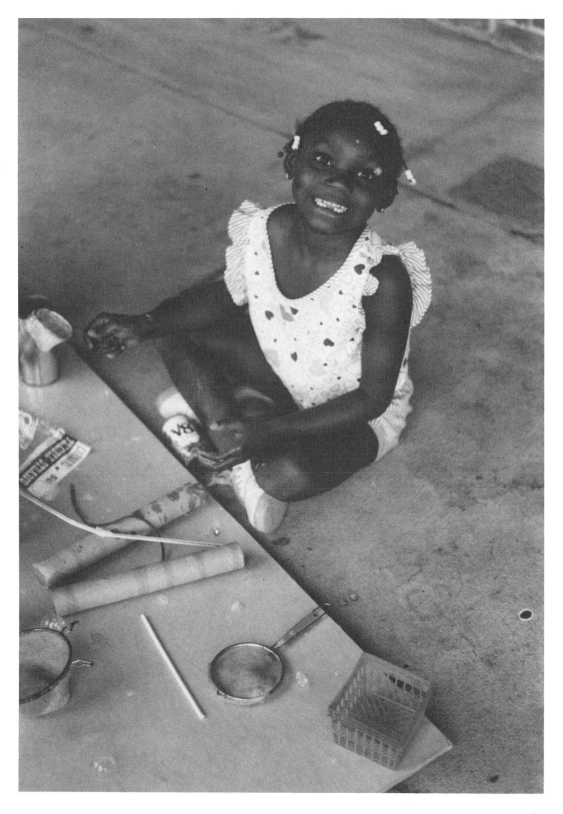

ACTIVITY 6
MAKING BUBBLES WITH HANDS

**What you
need**

Bubble solution
Plastic containers
Tables, blocks, *or* boxes
Drawing materials

**How you
begin**

Provide children with bubble solution. Children may have discovered that they can make bubbles with their wet hands by interlacing their fingers and rapidly hitting their palms together. One child found that he could make bubbles by making a circle with his thumb and index finger, dripping them in bubble solution, and blowing slowly through the circle.

Communicating

Encourage *communication* by asking children,

How did you make the bubbles with your hand? Show us what you did.

How did you make the small bubbles? Show us how you did that.

How did you make the big bubbles? Tell us how you did that so we can make big bubbles.

Five-year-old children may want to draw pictures to show how they made bubbles. These pictures can be put in a class book to share with parents.

THOUGHTS ON BLOWING BUBBLES

Give children the opportunity to blow bubbles often throughout the year. The possibilities for learning about bubbles are endless, and children will continually make new discoveries.

USING OUR BODIES IN SPACE

Young children spend their waking moments in some kind of motion. It is through movement that they learn about space. Children learn that more space is needed for some activities than for others. It takes more space to play hide and seek than it does to play house. Large objects occupy more space than small objects. Children are small and take up less space than adults. The purpose of these activities is to heighten children's awareness of space and to help them learn more about their bodies in space.

Science processes

Children use *space/time relations* as they move through space and discover how much space their bodies and body parts occupy. They make *predictions* about the amount of space needed for their bodies and body parts. *Measurement* is used to determine the accuracy of their predictions. Children *observe* carefully the space occupied by themselves and their classmates. From their explorations in space, children make *inferences* about the size of the spaces needed for small and large body parts. Children *communicate* their discoveries and plan together spaces that are large enough to accommodate several children. Understandings necessary for *classification* and seriation are developed as children look for spaces that are alike and *compare* those that are different from each other. Children draw *conclusions* about space from their varied experiences.

ACTIVITY 1
OUTLINING BODIES

**What you
need**

Colored chalk
Rope—several lengths
String *or* yarn
Glue
Paper—large sheets

**How you
begin**

In this activity you draw around children's bodies and body parts. You can use different colored chalk to draw on rugs or tile surfaces. Classroom furniture can be moved to provide sufficient space. You can also do the activity outdoors using several lengths of rope to outline the children. This activity should be carried out with a small group of children.

To begin, while they are standing, ask them to make themselves as tall as they can; then to make themselves as small as they can. Typically, children will stand on their tiptoes to make themselves tall, and squat with their heads between their knees to make themselves small.

Now tell the children to lie flat on their backs on the floor and make themselves as small as they can with their arms and legs against their bodies. With a colored piece of chalk draw around the children's bodies. This will result in oval shapes. Then ask the children to stretch their arms and legs out while you draw around them again with a different colored piece of chalk.

**Observing and
inferring**

Tell the children to stand up and *look at* the chalk marks that were drawn around their bodies. Encourage the children to make *inferences* by asking,

> Which space is bigger? The space inside the [color] chalk or the space inside the [color] chalk?
> Were the children's legs and arms by their sides? Stretched out? Why do you think so?

Children have commented: "I'm bigger when I stretch." "The space is bigger when we stretch out." "Look how big I am." "This is the smallest space. Our arms are beside us." "I want to draw around my hand."

Observing and using spatial relations

Tell the children you will draw around different parts of their bodies. They can stretch out on the floor inside their space and you will draw around their arms and legs. Tell them to *observe* the chalk marks drawn around their arms and legs. Encourage the use of *spatial relations* by asking,

Which takes up more floor space? Arms? Legs?
Do they take up the same amount of space? How can you be sure?

Measuring and comparing

Encourage the children to *measure* the spaces with string or yarn and *compare* (basis for seriation) the lengths of the two pieces:

Which string is longer—the one from the space for your arm or the one for your leg?

In one kindergarten five-year-olds compared the pieces of yarn with their own arms and legs.

Have the children draw around other parts of their bodies with your help or that of other children. In one nursery school three- and four-year-olds drew around each other's hands, feet, fingers, elbows, toes (shoes off), knees, and noses. Provide string and yarn so that children can measure and compare body parts.

Predicting

To encourage the children to predict, say

Which parts take up more floor space? The nose or elbow? The hand or foot? The finger or toe?

Children can keep the string or yarn showing the length of their body parts and glue them on a large piece of paper. Each part can be labeled for the children. Allow children to continue this activity as long as they are interested.

ACTIVITY 2
FITTING CARDBOARD PIECES

What you need

Cardboard cut into large and small rectangles, squares, and circles. (Cardboard box tops *or* tag board may be used.)

How you begin

Cut cardboard into assorted shapes to approximate the sizes of the children's body parts.

Predicting and using spatial relations

Hold up the smallest piece of cardboard and ask,

Which one of your body parts will fit in this space?

Discuss the children's answers, and allow each child to try the *predicted* body part. Ask questions to encourage the use of *spatial relations*:

Does your _____ fit in the space?
Are there any other body parts that can fit in this space?

Three- and four-year-olds found that their noses, finger tips, and elbows fit in the same space.

Observing and communicating

Place the various cardboard pieces on the floor, and tell the children to find the spaces that fit their body parts. Let children explore the spaces indicated by the cardboard pieces. Talk with the children about their discoveries and encourage them to *share* what they find out with each other.

Using spatial relations

One child couldn't find a piece of cardboard to fit his body. He put several pieces together and lay down. He realized the cardboard was too big for him and removed two pieces. Then he chose four smaller pieces and lay down again. This time the pieces fit and he asked the teacher to help him tape them together.

Concluding

Five-year-olds have drawn the following *conclusions* about space: "Both hands fit in the same space." "Feet take up more space than hands." "Some of our bodies take up more space than others." "It takes less floor space to sit up than to lie down." "Most parts of the body fit best in rectangular spaces than in squares and circles." "Heads and noses fit in circular spaces."

166

How investigation continues Allow children to use the cardboard pieces as long as they are interested. They may want to put several pieces together to represent themselves.

ACTIVITY 3
EXPLORING BOXES

What you need

Variety of boxes—shoe, furniture, grocery, and office supplies

Knife *or* other tool for cutting cardboard

How you begin

Provide children with an assortment of boxes. Several boxes should be tall so that children can stand inside them. Make a door in the tall boxes by vertically cutting along one side. Children can open the door and go inside the box.

Classifying

Show a shoe box to the children and ask,

> What shape is this box?
> How many sides does it have?
> Does it take up space? On the floor? In the air?

Discuss the children's answers, and help them to develop understandings for *classification* by asking them to find other boxes that are the same size as the box.

Predicting

Ask the children,

> What part of your body would fit in this box?

Have them try to fit the *predicted* body part in the box:

> Does your _____ fit in the box?
> Is it larger than the box? Smaller? The same size?
> What other parts of your body will fit in the box?

Children's answers have been as follows: "I can get both hands in the box." "My feet and hands are in the box." "It is too big for my hand." "It is too little for my leg." "It's too small for my head." "Jim and I can get both our hands in the box." Allow the children to explore all the boxes. Talk about the amount of space they occupy:

> Your arm fits when you lay it flat. Will your arm fit if you hold it up straight?
> Can you lie down in the box? Stand up?
> Can you find a box that your body will fit in when you stand up?

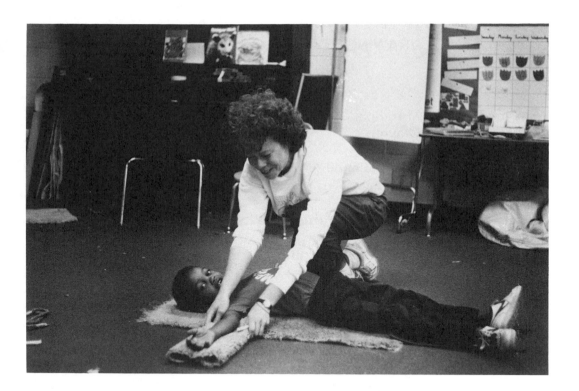

Communicating   Children especially enjoy the tall boxes when they can walk inside. They begin to think of themselves as occupying space. Encourage children to *share* ideas and plan space explorations together. Plans children have made and accomplished together are discovering how many children can squat, stand, and lie down in the same box; walking across the floor with a foot in each box; moving with hands, feet, elbows, knees, or head in boxes; and sitting in boxes and moving across the room.

Comparing   You can ask the children to look at the house center and consider:

> Which furniture takes up more space? Less space?
> Can you think of a way to change the furniture?

The children in one kindergarten changed the furniture until they were satisfied with the arrangement. The teacher was careful not to suggest that any of the arrangements produced more space.

ACTIVITY 4
DRAWING SPACES

What you need

Mural paper (butcher paper)
Crayons

How you begin

Provide mural paper and crayons for the children to use in drawing spaces to fit their body parts.

Predicting and using spatial relations

Have the children choose a sheet of mural paper and a crayon. Then ask them to draw a space on the paper in which they think their hand will fit. Observe the children as they draw and fit their hands in the spaces. Were all of the children successful? If not, what problems did they have? Next ask the children to draw a space that their feet will fit. Encourage the use of *spatial relations* by asking the children,

Will your foot fit in the space you drew?
Is the space too big? Too small?
Can you think of any other part of your body that would fit in the space?

How investigation continues

Some children may want to draw a space for their whole bodies. This is more difficult since children cannot view their bodies in the same way they can their body parts. Looking at themselves in a full-length mirror sometimes helps them to be more accurate. Children may draw spaces big enough for themselves and their friends. This activity is very popular with children.

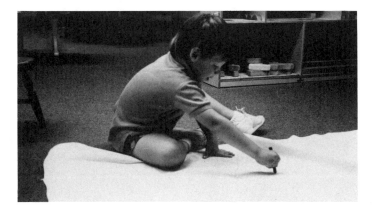

ACTIVITY 5
MOVING IN SPACE

How you begin

Tell the children to look at the open space in the classroom. Ask them,

Is there enough space for all of you to walk?

Predicting and using spatial relations

Discuss the children's answers with them. Children have responded: "No, push the chairs back more." "Yes, if we walk side by side." "Sure, you can walk in a line." "We can walk slowly." Have the children walk in the space several times using their ideas. Then ask them,

Did you have enough space?

Talk about the children's answers and ask,

Do you think you have enough space to run?

One kindergarten child said, "Let's take turns. We'll run into each other."

Comparing

Follow the children's suggestions and talk about the results. Ask the children,

Did you need more space when you walked or ran?

Most children will say they needed more space to run. One four-year-old child said, "You need lots of space to run," and a five-year-old said, "You put your legs and arms out to run. You need more space."

Observing and inferring

Tell the children to lie on their backs and move across the room. Then ask,

Did you move fast? Slowly? Why?

Now tell the children to move across the room on their stomachs. Then ask,

Did you move fast? Slowly? Why?
Did you move as fast as you did on your backs? Why?

Tell the children to move on their backs without using their legs. Then tell them to move on their stomachs without using their arms. Ask,

171

Was there enough space?
Did you move faster or slower under the different circumstances?

How investigation continues   Encourage the children to think of different ways to move in space. Children have suggested: "Hop." "Jump." "Move with your hands over your head." "Move on your side." "Move on your back without using your arms or legs." If possible, explore each child's idea with the children.

ACTIVITY 6
MAKING FOOTPRINTS

What you need

Mural paper (butcher paper)—long sheets *or* tape several short sheets together
Tempera paint—various colors
Wide brushes
Jars of water

How you begin

Provide mural paper, brushes, containers of tempera paints, and jars of water. Say,

> When you run your feet move very fast, and when you walk they move more slowly.
> Take off your shoes and socks. I'm going to paint your feet with a brush, and let you walk across the mural paper.
> After you walk across the paper, I'll put paint on your feet again, and let you run across another sheet of paper.

Observing and comparing

Paint the children's feet and let them walk the length of the paper. They will *observe* that their footprints become lighter and lighter as they move across the paper. Paint the children's feet again in the same color or a different color and ask them to run across a second sheet of paper. When the paint dries, place the children's papers next to each other, and ask the children,

> Are there longer spaces between your footprints when you walk or when you run? Why?
> Count your footprints. Do you touch the floor more often when you run or walk?
> Do you use as much floor space when you run as when you walk?

Discuss the children's answers. Encourage children to think of other movements to record on paper. Suggestions children have made are "hopping," "jumping," "galloping," and "do a bear walk—walking on hands and feet."

THOUGHTS ON USING OUR BODIES IN SPACE

Continue throughout the year to explore space with children. They learn what their bodies can do in space and how to relate them to other objects in space. Throwing objects at targets, completing obstacle courses, and moving bodies to music develop spatial awareness.

WORKING WITH WOOD

Children are fascinated by wood and tools. They receive a great deal of satisfaction from nailing two pieces of wood together. It is not necessary to name the resulting form; it is enough to drive the nail well enough to hold the wood together. Most programs for young children include working with wood. Often the emphasis in woodworking is placed on skill in using tools, and the opportunity for problem solving is minimized. Through experimentation and teacher guidance, children can learn the properties of wood and the effects of different tools on wood. They can plan constructions and choose their materials and tools to carry out their plans. Woodworking involves such a variety of skills, tools, and materials that the opportunities for using the processes of science are unlimited.

Science processes

Understandings necessary for *classification* are developed as children find out that some woods are softer and easier to cut and drive a nail through than other woods. Children make *comparisons* (basis for seriation) between nails and pieces of wood to determine which ones to use in their constructions. *Space/time relations* are used as children figure out how to saw wood and how to nail pieces so they will stay together. *Measurement* is used when children place pieces of wood together to find out which one is longer. String and yarn are used to mark the desired length and/or width of a piece of wood. Children make *inferences* about why wood cracks and nails protrude from wood. They make *predictions* about how their finished constructions will look. They *communicate* their *observations* about woodworking through verbalizations and demonstrations of what they have learned. Children draw *conclusions* about woodworking such as "A large nail will split a thin piece of wood" and "It takes two nails to stop wood from turning."

What you need for wood activities

Workbench—child size

Tool cabinet or pegboard to hang tools

Wood scraps (white pine, yellow pine, spruce, oak)—sources are construction sites, cabinet makers, lumber companies, and home workshops.

Claw hammers—child size

Nails—1¼" (3.2 cm) roofing nails with large head, 3-penny common, 4-penny common, 3-penny finishing with flat head

Vise attached to workbench

C-clamp—4"

Sandpaper—coarse (80 grit), medium (120–150 grit), fine (150–240 grit).

Saws—several coping saws and blades, two 16" (41.5 cm) crosscut saws, one 10" (25.5 cm) hack saw

Hand drill and bits up to ¼" (.64 cm)

Brace and bits—¼" (.64 cm), ⅜" (.97 cm), ½" (1.3 cm), ¾" (1.92 cm)

Screwdrivers—3" (7.6 cm), 4" (10 cm)

Screws—flat head wood screw #6 in lengths 1" (2.5 cm)–1½" (3.8 cm)

Pliers

ACTIVITY 1
LEARNING ABOUT WOOD

What you need

Workbench with vise
Wood scraps
Hammers
Nails
Small containers
Three different colored boxes for wood scraps
Three different colored boxes for nails

How you begin

In a container near the workbench, place an assortment of wood scraps. These should represent various sizes and types of wood. White pine (soft), yellow pine or spruce (moderately soft), and oak (hard) are good choices. Hammers and small containers with at least three types of nails (large and small heads) should be on or near the workbench. Woodworking is so popular with children that they naturally gravitate to the workbench. You may want to limit the number of children working at the workbench to three or four.

Most first attempts at woodworking consist of hammering nails into wood or hammering two pieces of wood together. A few children may have difficulty driving a nail in wood. They hit the nails at an angle rather than straight on the head. You or another child can demonstrate how to hit a nail. Show children how to put wood in a vise. Sometimes it is easier to drive a nail in wood that is held steady by a vise. It may take several weeks before children succeed in using nails and hammers without difficulty.

Comparing

Encourage children to make *comparisons* between and among the varieties of wood and nails by asking the children:

Which wood is hardest to drive a nail in?
Which wood is easiest?
Why do you think you are having trouble hitting the nail? Can you find a nail with a bigger head? Smaller head?
Was the nail longer than your piece of wood?
Can you find a piece of wood that is wider than this one?

Three- and four-year-olds have commented while working with wood as follows: "I need a long nail for this big [thick] piece." "My nail went through the wood." "I nailed two pieces of wood together." "My nail won't go in the wood. This wood is tough" (hard). "My wood is skinny. I need a little nail." "It's easy to use this wood" (soft).

Classifying

It is easier for children to work with wood when they can find the kind of wood that they need quickly. When children are familiar with the terms "hard" and "soft" wood, help them develop understandings necessary for *classification*. Give them three different colored boxes, and ask them to put each kind of wood in a different box. After the children have sorted the wood ask,

> Is all the wood in the _____ box hard? In the _____ box soft?
> In the _____ box between hard and soft? How do you know?

One five-year-old child pointed to a box of soft wood and said, "There is hard wood in the soft wood box." The teacher asked, "How can you be sure it's hard wood?" The child said, "I'll test it with a nail." The children tested all of the wood with nails and discovered that a few pieces of wood were placed in the wrong boxes. They learned that they could not always depend on their sense of sight and touch for accuracy. Encourage children to sort the nails in three boxes. In this case they can depend on their sense of sight.

ACTIVITY 2
BUILDING STRUCTURES

What you need

Workbench with vise
Wood scraps sorted into three different colored boxes
Hammers
Nails sorted into three different colored boxes
Sandpaper

How you begin

Provide children with the same materials as in activity 1 plus several sheets of fine to coarse sandpaper. As children experiment with wood and tools, they make discoveries that later enable them to build more complicated structures. They learn that a nail can go through wood and stick to the workbench. At first children may try to pull wood up with their hands. One child said, "This is hard. I can't do it," and another child said, "That's easy." He used the claw end of the hammer to remove the wood.

Measuring

Through experimentation children discover that they must *measure* nails against wood if they want to avoid nailing wood to the workbench. They measure nails against two pieces of wood to determine if a nail is long enough to go in the second piece.

Concluding

Children find out if they put two pieces of wood together with one nail it will rotate on the nail. A second nail will stop the wood from turning. One five-year-old girl tried to connect two pieces of wood in a T fashion. She could not put the nail through both pieces of wood to hold them together. She solved the problem by nailing a piece of wood on the back of the boards at the point where they met. From their experimentations one group of children discovered the following: "Nails that go through the wood can be hammered back into the wood." "Bent nails can't be used again." "Hitting bent nails with a hammer may make them straight." "It is easier to hit big nail heads than small ones." "Some wood is thick and some is thin." "If you nail a big nail in a skinny piece of wood, the wood will crack."

Using spatial relations and inferring

You can help children explore *spatial relations* and make *inferences* about their constructions by asking questions and making comments about their work:

178

Why do you think the small piece of wood fell off?

Why do you think the wood split?

Look at the nail. Why do you think it won't go into the wood?

You put four pieces of wood together to make your construction. Why do you think it fell apart? How can you make it stay together?

Inferring

Give children fine, medium, and coarse sandpaper to remove splinters from their constructions. (Glue sandpaper around blocks of wood to make it easier for children to use.) Allow children to choose the kind of sandpaper they want to use. They will discover that the effectiveness of the sandpaper depends on the kind of wood and the type of paper. Ask questions such as

Why did you choose the fine sandpaper?

What kind of sandpaper do you think you need for that piece of wood?

One five-year-old child said, "I'm going to use the coarse sandpaper on my wood so I won't get splinters." Another child said, "Sandpaper is made out of sand, paper, and glue. I know why you sand." The teacher asked, "Why do you think we use sandpaper?" The child said, "To get splinters out." The teacher asked, "What is the material that you get when you use sandpaper?" He replied, "Little pieces of wood that come off."

179

ACTIVITY 3
USING SAWS

What you need

Workbench with vise *or* C-clamp
Wood scraps sorted into three different colored boxes
Yarn, string, *or* strips of paper
Pencils

How you begin

Two nursery school children were at the woodworking center. One little girl was sawing, and the other little girl asked her, "Why are you sawing?" She answered, "Because I haven't done it before." The addition of saws to the woodworking center offers children a new challenge. It is necessary to place wood in a vise or C-clamp to hold it in place. Sawing wood without a vise is never safe. Young children initially may prefer coping saws to larger saws. You should show inexperienced children how to put wood in a vise, hold the saw, and make a cut in the wood. Children will practice sawing wood until they are satisfied with their accomplishments.

Observing

Encourage children to *observe* what is happening as they saw by asking questions:

> What happens if you use the tip of the saw? If you saw straight? If you saw at an angle?
> Is it better to use long or short strokes?
> How does the blade feel after you saw?
> Why is there sawdust on the ground?

Children learn through experimentation that wood may crack if you saw too fast and that even strokes are more effective than broken strokes. One five-year-old learned that if he sawed too fast the wood broke off. He discovered that the saw blade was hot and that sawing produces sawdust just as sandpaper does. Another child wanted to saw a straight line so he decided to draw a line on the wood and follow it with the saw. While he was sawing the wood, the wood cracked so he decided to saw slower. In this instance, the child solved two problems: how to cut in a straight line and how to saw without cracking the wood.

Comparing

Help children to *compare* saws and wood (essential to seriation) as they work:

Which saw is heavier? Lighter?
Which one is easier to use with hard wood? Soft wood?
Which one is best to saw thick wood? Thin wood?

Measuring

Often children want to make something with two pieces of wood that are the same length. They may place two uneven pieces of wood together and draw a line along the shorter piece. They must saw on the line in order to have wood the correct length. Another way to assure that two pieces of wood are the same length is to *measure* them. Encourage children to use a single unit of measurement like a piece of yarn or string, or strip of paper. Ask questions such as

How can you remember how long you want the wood?
What can you use to measure the wood?

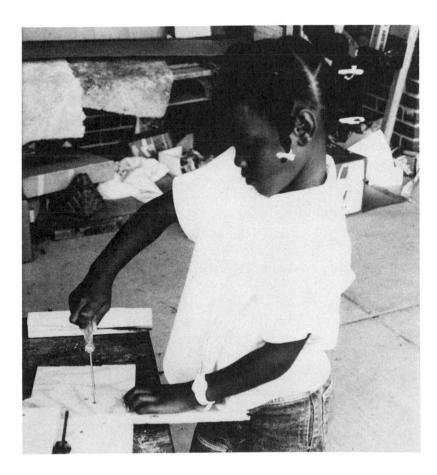

ACTIVITY 4
DRILLING HOLES FOR SCREWS

What you need

Workbench with vise
Wood scraps sorted into three different colored boxes
Hand drill and bits
Brace and bits
Screws
Screwdrivers
Hammers

How you begin

Provide the children with screws, screwdrivers, a hand drill, and a brace and bit. Most children will prefer to continue using the hand drill until they are familiar with drilling holes in wood.

Predicting

At first children will explore making holes with the various bits. Encourage children to *predict* the size hole each bit will make.

> Will the holes be the same size as the bits?
> Will this bit make a larger hole than that bit?
> Which bit will make the smallest hole? The largest hole?

Observing and comparing

Children will discover that they must select a bit smaller in diameter than the screw they plan to use or the screw will come out of the hole. This requires careful *observation* and *comparison* of the bit with the screw.

How investigation continues

Children may try to hammer screws in wood. They will find that hammering screws is difficult and that drilling holes for screws and screwing them into wood with a screwdriver is more satisfactory. Some children may want to screw two pieces of wood together. This means that each board will need a screw hole. One five-year-old child's bit was too short to go through both boards. He stacked the boards and drilled until the bit had gone through the first board and had made a mark on the second board. He took off the top board and finished drilling the second board. Children may encounter other problems to solve while using drills and bits. You should encourage them, whenever possible, to solve their own problems.

ACTIVITY 5
ADDING TO STRUCTURES

What you need

Workbench with vise
Hammers
Brace and bits
Hand drill and bits
Screws
Screwdrivers
Sandpaper
Carpet scraps
Roof shingles
Cloth pieces

Wood scraps sorted into three different colored boxes
Nails sorted into three different colored boxes
Plastic jar with bottle tops
Metal jar with bottle tops
Plastic tops from detergent bottles
Manila drawing paper
Felt-tip markers and/or crayons

How you begin

After children have become well acquainted with hammering nails and using saws, drills, and screwdrivers in making constructions, offer them interesting things to use for decoration. These may include metal and plastic bottle and jar tops, carpet squares, and pieces of cloth.

Observing

At first children will experiment by choosing materials at random and nailing or screwing them to wood. Encourage careful *observation* and experimentation with the materials by asking the children questions:

Which materials are hard? Soft?
What are the materials made of?
Where do you think they came from?
How could you use the plastic tops? The jar tops? The carpet squares?

One five-year-old chose a metal jar top to hammer into a piece of wood. He said, "It will take me a long time to hammer this in." The teacher asked, "Why do you think so?" He replied, "Because the wood has metal on it." The kindergarten and nursery school children discovered that if they nailed a jar top on a piece of wood, the jar top would rotate on the wood. It took two nails to stop the jar top from turning. They also found that jar tops make good wheels, but work better if the tops are the same size.

Predicting and communicating

Many children become planners and search for the pieces of wood and materials they want before driving the first nail. Some children will be able to *predict* what their constructions will look like by *drawing* pictures of them. Children typically make crosses, spaceships, planes, boats, cars, trucks, and other transportation toys. Other constructions children have made are cameras, walkie-talkies, bookcases, furniture, houses, signs, and the letters T and H.

Concluding Children draw *conclusions* throughout their woodworking experiences. Some conclusions children have expressed are the following: "Woodworking is fun." "Nails with big heads are easier to hit." "Constructions need to be sandpapered." "It takes two nails to stop wood from turning." "Some wood is too hard to use."

THOUGHTS ON WORKING WITH WOOD

Woodworking should be carried out with children indoors or outdoors throughout the year. With more experience children gain expertise in using tools, and their structures become more original and complex.

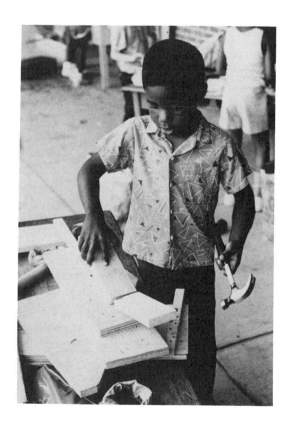

MAKING TOYS

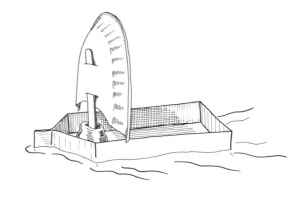

Children play with toys every day. Usually their experiences are with commercial toys bought at a store or through a toy manufacturer. A few children have played with handmade toys made by a parent or friend. Often children are unaware that toys can be made at home or school with everyday materials. They have had little or no opportunity to make toys themselves. Making toys gives children the opportunity to use what they have learned about the properties of materials and the different ways to combine them to make various objects. It also helps them to appreciate the planning and problem solving necessary to make a toy that is functional and enjoyable.

Science processes

Children *observe* materials closely and make *inferences* about the kinds of materials to use to make a specific toy. *Space/time relations* are developed as children arrange and rearrange materials to their satisfaction. They use *measurement* to assure that parts of toys fit together properly. They *predict* how their toys will look and how they can use them in the various centers. They *describe* the characteristics of their handmade toys and *classify* them as satisfactory or unsatisfactory. From their experiences with making toys, children draw *conclusions* about how to make toys that are fun to play with and durable.

How you prepare

Begin making toys with small groups of children toward the end of the year. Children need an adult readily available to help them plan and carry out their plans. You may want to choose different classroom centers from those described in the activities. Although three centers are discussed, toys can be made over a long period of time to include every center. In preparation for making toys, send notes home asking parents to bring in those items from the list below that are not available in your classroom.

What you need for toys activities

Supplies children are likely to request to use in making toys:

Bean seeds
Bottle caps
Buttons
Cardboard
Clothespins
Corks
Cotton balls
Crayons
Glue
Milk cartons
Nails
Paper bags
Paper plates
Pine cones
Play dough
Screws
String
Tin cans
Toothpicks
Wallpaper
Wood
Yarn balls

Aluminum pie pans
Boxes—variety of sizes
Burlap, monk's cloth, *or* other fabric plastic needles will go through
Cardboard rollers or tubes
Construction paper
Contact paper—clear
Cups—plastic, paper, and Styrofoam
Frozen food aluminum and plastic dishes
Jar lids—plastic and metal
Moist clay (self-hardening)
Plastic containers—all kinds
Popsicle sticks
Spools of thread *or* empty spools
Typewriter ribbon spools—empty
Carpet squares
Felt-tip markers
Pipe cleaners

Equipment children may need in making toys:

Children's plastic needles *or* rag-rug plastic needles
Scissors
Woodworking tools
Workbench

ACTIVITY 1
INTRODUCING HANDMADE TOYS

What you need

Handmade toys as examples
Strips of paper for names
Box
Chart paper
Felt-tip marker

How you begin

To introduce the first activity, say to the children,

> We have many toys in our classroom. What is a toy?

Most children will define a toy as something "to play with" or "fun to play with." Ask the children,

> Where do we get toys?

One three-year-old child said, "Santa Claus brings them," and a four-year-old said, "Buy them at the store." The teacher asked, "What if there were no stores to buy toys?" The children answered: "Build a doll house." "Bring boxes from the attic and play with the toys." "Build a store." "Make toys." After the children have talked about ways to acquire toys, show them several homemade toys. Cloth and wooden toys should be represented. Handmade toys that have been used with children are stuffed cloth dolls and animals, wooden animals and transportation toys, paper and cloth puppets, corn husk dolls and animals, and pine cone people and animals. Ask the children,

> What kind of toys are these?

Discuss the children's answers, and point out that the word "handmade" means to make something with the hands. Toys can be handmade instead of bought at a store.

Observing and inferring

Tell the children to *observe* the handmade toys closely and encourage them to make *inferences* about how they were made. One four-year-old described the way she thought a doll was made: "Cut the clothes out. Stuff them with cotton. Sew them up. Paint eyes, nose, and mouth. Put yarn hair on. Dress her up."

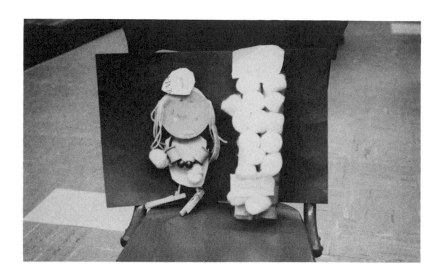

Explain to the children that instead of buying toys, they are going to make toys for some of the classroom centers. Choose children who will be in the first group to make toys by drawing six to eight names out of a box. Tell the other children they will all have a turn to make a toy later.

With the children who have been selected, go and look at the water play center. Ask,

> What additional toys would you like that would make water play more interesting?

Five-year-old children have suggested boats, amphibian planes, sieves, and balls for the center; three- and four-year-olds were interested in making "all kinds of boats."

Classifying

Discuss the toys that the children want to make. Ask them,

> What materials will you need to make your toys?

In order to make that decision, children must mentally *classify* materials as satisfactory and unsatisfactory to use in making their toys. Make a list of the toys the children plan to make and the materials they will need. Materials children have suggested are paper cups, aluminum and plastic dishes and pans, gallon plastic bottles, cloth, carpet squares, milk cartons, wood and woodworking tools, moist clay, and cardboard tubes. The next day have the materials available for the children.

ACTIVITY 2
MAKING TOYS FOR THE WATER PLAY CENTER

What you need

Variety of large boxes covered with contact paper
Materials requested by children and necessary equipment
Manila drawing paper
Felt-tip markers and/or crayons

How you begin

Provide a variety of large boxes covered with contact paper and the materials mentioned by the children in activity 1.

Classifying

In order to help children find materials easily and develop understandings for *classification,* ask them to help you put the materials that are alike in one of the boxes. Continue this activity until the boxes are filled with the separated materials. Talk about the sources of each material:

> Did it come from the carpenter shop? The grocery store? The hardware store? The drugstore?

Ask the children questions about the properties of the materials:

> Which materials are hard? Soft?
> Will they fall apart in water?
> Will the material float?
> What shape is it?
> Can it be cut? Sawed? Drilled?
> Can it be sandpapered?

Predicting and communicating

Ask each child,

> What toy are you going to make?
> What materials will you need?

Don't be surprised if children decide to make toys that are different from the ones named the day before. Encourage the children to *predict* how their toys will look by *drawing* pictures of them, but not all children will want to draw pictures.

How you continue

Discuss the pictures and/or plans with the children, and when needed, assist them in making their toys. Allow them, however, to decide what materials to use and how to put them together.

Observing and inferring

Children will learn through experience that sometimes their toys need to be changed in some way to work satisfactorily. One three-year-old child chose a cardboard roller to make a boat. The teacher asked, "How will you make the boat?" He said, "I'll color it. Then I'll put a red piece of paper on for a sail." The teacher said, "Tell me if you need help." The child made the boat without difficulty and put it in the water. He played with the boat until it sank. He showed it to the teacher and said, "My boat sank. It got wet." The teacher asked, "What do you think you should do?" He replied, "Make a boat with something else." The teacher helped him put various materials in the water to find out whether or not they would sink. The child chose a plastic dessert dish, a Popsicle stick, and a piece of cloth to make his second boat. He was satisfied with the results since the boat stayed afloat.

Communicating and using time relations

When the children have finished making their toys, ask them to *describe* them and demonstrate their use. Encourage using *time relations* by asking the children,

> What was the first thing that you did to make your toy? The second?
> What did you do last?

Comments children have made and questions they have asked each other about water toys are as follows: "How did you nail the sail on?" "Was it hard to drill the holes?" "That's a neat boat. Can I play with it?" "I made a boat like that one." "Are you going to put the sieve in the water center?" "I'm going to make a toy like that one." Encourage the children to play with their toys in the water center and to allow the other children to play with them.

What the children made

The following are examples of water toys children have made for a water center (their ages are identified):

Sailboat—A narrow piece of wood was nailed perpendicular to a rectangular piece of wood. A cloth sail was nailed to the upright piece of wood. Five-year-old.

Sailboat—A milk carton was cut in half lengthwise. A decorated paper plate sail was glued to the inside. Three-year-old.

191

Raft—Piece of wood with a smaller piece nailed in the middle for a cabin. Four-year-old.

"Three Men in a Tub"—Three figures were drawn, colored, and cut from manila drawing paper. They were glued to a plastic container and named "Three Men in a Tub." Five-year-old.

Sieve—Holes were drilled in a thin piece of wood. Four wooden pieces were nailed upright around the wood for sides. Five-year-old.

Ball—Aluminum foil ball. Air spaces kept ball afloat for a few days, but it eventually sank. Later newspaper was placed in a sandwich bag and sealed with masking tape. This worked much better. Four-year-old.

Sieve—Holes were drilled in the inside of a plastic container. Sharp drill holes on the outside were smoothed down with a hammer. Three-year-old.

Plane—Two pieces of wood were nailed together. A small piece of wood was nailed on top for the cabin, and a piece of wood was nailed across the back end for a tail. Two spools were nailed on for motors. Five-year-old.

Unsatisfactory toys—Boats made of earth clay and play dough and left to dry sank when they were then put in water. The children decided to make wooden boats.

ACTIVITY 3
MAKING TOYS FOR THE HOUSE CENTER

What you need

Chart paper
Felt-tip markers and/or crayons
Materials requested by children and necessary equipment
Variety of large boxes covered with contact paper
Manila drawing paper

How you begin

Select a second small group of children to make toys. Tell them that they can make toys for the house center. Examine the house center with the children, and talk about the toys in the center. Ask the children,

> Can you think of toys that would make our center more interesting?

Three-, four-, and five-year-olds have suggested food, dolls, puppets, dishes, place mats, stuffed animals, baby blankets, and cameras.

Classifying

Discuss the toys that the children plan to make. Ask them,

> What materials will you need to make your toys?

Make a list of the toys the children plan to make and the materials they will need. Materials that children have suggested are cardboard rollers, wood, Popsicle sticks, moist clay, yarn, cotton balls, boxes, construction paper, clothespins, spools, plastic needles, play dough, pipe cleaners, cloth, and plastic containers. The next day provide the materials and the large boxes in which to sort them.

In order to develop understandings for *classification*, tell the children to help you put the materials that are alike in one of the boxes. Continue this activity until the boxes are filled with the separated materials. Talk about the source of each of the materials.

> Did it come from the grocery store? Fabric shop? Carpenter shop? Art store?

Ask the children questions about the properties of the materials:

> Which materials can you fold? Squeeze? Twist? Break? What shape are the materials?

193

Which materials can be cut? Sawed? Drilled?
Which materials are soft? Hard?

Predicting and communicating

Ask each child,

What toy are you going to make?
What material will you need?

Encourage children to *predict* how their toys will look by *drawing* pictures of them. Discuss the pictures and/or plans with the children, and when needed, assist them in making their toys.

Communicating and using time relations

When children have finished making their toys, ask them to *describe* them and demonstrate their use. Encourage using *time relations* by asking the children,

What was the first thing you did to make your toy? The second?
What did you do last?

Comments children have made and questions they have asked about each other's toys are as follows: "How did you make the place mats the same size?" "The blanket is a little crooked, but it won't matter." "I like your puppet." "Can we play with the food?" "I'm glad you made a bear for us." "You sew good." "That looks like a real camera."

What the children made

The following are examples of toys children have made for house centers (their ages are identified):

Toy for the stuffed cat—Three spools were glued across the top of a narrow box. A pipe cleaner was glued across the top of the spools, and a small yarn ball was glued on top of the pipe cleaner and each spool. Three-year-old.

Doll with blond hair—An oatmeal box top was used for the head and yellow yarn for the hair. Features were drawn with crayons. The hat and body were made of construction paper. Arms and legs were made of pipe cleaners. Cotton balls were used for hands and clothespins for feet. Around the neck was a pipe cleaner necklace strung with spools and beads. Five-year-old.

Furry bear—Two paper towel rollers were glued together and covered with cotton balls. A face was cut from manila paper and glued to the top of the roller. Features were drawn with crayons. Five-year-old.

Place mats—To make them the same size, the child made one and then drew around it three times on construction paper. Four-year-old.

Baby blanket—The child cut monk's cloth to the size wanted. The teacher helped the child turn down the edges and pin them. The child sewed them with a plastic needle and yarn. Five-year-old.

Unsatisfactory toys—Any toy put together with tape soon fell apart. They were put back together with glue.

ACTIVITY 4
MAKING TOYS FOR THE BLOCK CENTER

**What you
need**

Chart paper
Felt-tip markers and/or crayons
Materials requested by children and necessary supplies
    and equipment
Variety of large boxes covered with contact paper
Manila drawing paper

**How you
begin**

In this activity have a small group of children make toys
for the block center. Carry out the activity in the same
manner as activities 2 and 3. Toys children have suggested making are dollhouses, bean bags, cars, trains,
trucks, spaceships, planes, and signs. Materials that children have said they needed are boxes, wood, spools, plastic and metal jar lids, string, yarn, plastic containers,
clothespins, pipe cleaners, corks, bean seeds, cloth, burlap, needles, and wallpaper.

Classifying

To encourage the development of understandings for
classification, you can ask the following questions about
the properties of the materials:

> Can the material be cut? Drilled? Sawed?
> What materials can be torn? Twisted? Folded? Squeezed?
> What shape are the materials?
> Which materials can be sewn together? How?

Comments children have made and questions they have
asked about each other's toys are as follows: "Can we make
furniture for the dollhouse?" "How many beans are in the
bean bag?" "The balance looks like fun." "I'm going to
make a spaceship." "You wrote 'stop' real well."

**What the
children made**

The following are examples of toys children have made for
a block center (their ages are identified):

Train—Two cardboard cartons were attached to each other
    by two long, narrow pieces of construction paper.
    Cotton balls were used for wheels. <u>Four-year-old.</u>
Spaceship—Two small cardboard cartons were glued on
    top of each other. A hole was made in the top of one
    carton for a clothespin. Pipe cleaners were wrapped

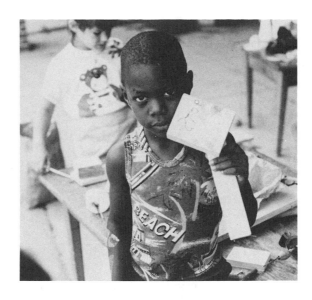

around the clothespin with a piece of colored cellophane attached for a flag. Four-year-old.

Stop sign—A small wooden square was nailed to one end of a small piece of wood. The word "stop" was written with a felt pen on the square piece of wood. Five-year-old.

Wooden plane—A plane was made by nailing a long and short piece of wood together. A piece of wood was nailed on one end for the cabin and two spools were nailed on the bottom for wheels. Five-year-old.

Dollhouse—Four boxes were glued together to make four rooms. A folded piece of cardboard was glued across the top boxes for a roof. Wallpaper was cut and glued inside each room. String was used to measure rooms for cutting paper the right size. The dollhouse didn't turn out perfectly, but the child was satisfied with the results. Five-year-old.

Bean bag—A small piece of construction paper was placed on a piece of burlap, and lines were drawn around it to mark the burlap for cutting. The procedure was repeated on another piece of burlap. The burlap pieces were cut on the lines. One piece of burlap was placed on top of the other, and three sides were sewn together with a plastic needle and yarn. The bag was filled with beans. The opening was sewn shut. Five-year-old.

ACTIVITY 5
REPAIRING HANDMADE TOYS

What you need

Supplies and equipment necessary to repair handmade toys

What you should look for

Observe the children as they play with the toys in the various centers. Do they prefer the handmade toys to the commercial toys? Do they lose interest in the toys easily? Are the children willing to let other children use the toys they have made? How do children play with the toys? Do they play with them in the way the toys suggest?

Classifying

A nursery school teacher observed that children moved toys from one center to another. The "wooden spaceship" was used at the water table as well as in the block center. Wooden trucks, planes, and cars moved from the water table to the block center and back again. Clay food was used in the house and block centers, and bean bags were popular outside. Some of the children commented that they had made "good" toys "'cause we can use them lots of places."

What you should look for

You should also notice the following: Are the toys sturdy or do they fall apart? Do children assume the responsibility of repairing a toy or making another toy? Can they think of another way to make the toy functional? In one kindergarten the teacher observed that the children preferred handmade toys to commercial toys as long as they were durable. If the toys tore or came apart, they no longer wanted to play with them.

Communicating and measuring

Sometimes children take toys to the children who made them and say, "Fix it." A few children respond by mending the toys themselves. When a plane fell apart, a nursery school child, who had made the plane, nailed it back together. Her comment was "The nail was too short."

Communicating and concluding

Often children bring a toy to the teacher and say, "Can you fix it?" or "Tell me what to do." A five-year-old complained that the paper place mats in the house center were torn. The teacher said, "That's too bad. Can they be fixed?" The child answered, "No, they're all torn up." The teacher said, "Let's ask Sue (the child who made the place mats) what to do." Sue said, "Paper mats tear." At group time the teacher presented the problem of the place mats to the group. Suggestions given by the children were the following: "Make them out of cloth." "Don't make them again. We don't need them." "Use paper doilies." "Make wooden ones." "Cover them with contact paper." After discussing the many possibilities given by the children, it was decided to cover construction paper with contact paper. The teacher helped Sue make the paper mats and cover them with contact paper. The place mats were sturdy and didn't tear again.

When there are problems with handmade toys, you should first ask the children who made the toys to solve the problems. Sometimes children are unable to offer solutions, and then the problem can be presented to the class. Practical suggestions children have given to improve toys are as follows: "Make smaller stitches when you sew the bean bag. The beans come out." "Use wet clay instead of play dough. It crumbles." "Put more glue on so the puppet's eyes won't fall off." "Use glue instead of masking tape." "Measure the place mats so they'll be the same size."

When to help solve problems

Sometimes you must intervene and suggest ways children can solve problems. A kindergarten class had a problem that none of the children could solve. The paint on the clay food rubbed off on their hands. They attempted to solve their problem by painting the food again, but the paint continued to come off. The teacher offered a solution. She asked, "Have you ever heard of shellac?" The children said, "No." The teacher explained that covering paint with shellac would keep it from coming off. The children used a brush dipped in shellac to cover the painted foods. When the shellac dried, the paint did not come off the food, and their problem was solved.

THOUGHTS ON MAKING TOYS

You should encourage children to think about materials and how they can be combined to make something durable. Children can be helped to develop the understandings to *predict, classify,* and use *space/time relations* by asking them to decide what they want to make, the kinds of materials they can use satisfactorily, and the best ways to put them together. Making toys can continue indoors and outdoors throughout the spring of the year.

ABOUT THE AUTHOR

Rosemary Althouse is a professor of Early Childhood Education at Winthrop College, Rock Hill, South Carolina. She is also the director of the Macfeat Early Childhood Laboratory School and former director of the Center of Excellence in Early Childhood Education, both at Winthrop College. She earned a B.S. from the University of Pennsylvania, an M.A. from State University of Iowa, and a Ph.D. from Florida State University. Dr. Althouse has published numerous articles in professional journals and is the coauthor of *Science Experiences for Young Children* and the author of *The Young Child: Learning with Understanding*, both published by Teachers College Press.